Dear Michael,
  I hope this book is
a blessing to you.

Endorsements

Jon Lineberger's story is a vivid example of the truth "You Can Begin Again." Jon writes with transparent honesty and with the hope that all who read this book will discover redemption in Christ and the new life our Savior provides. I celebrate the grace of God in Jon Lineberger's life and pray this story will capture your heart and lead you to the one who changes lives.

Dr. Jack Graham
Pastor, Prestonwood Baptist Church

Change is possible and Jon Lineberger's painfully transparent yet ultimately victorious story and truths to a changed life in Christ will bring hope to multitudes that God can and will work in the lives of people when they humbly submit to Jesus Christ. I appreciate that this book is not directly about Jon, but the love, grace, and hope offered in a sincere relationship with Jesus Christ. God continues to perform miracles in the lives of people every day.

Dr. Paul Meier
Founder, Meier Clinics
Author of over 80 books

If ever someone is looking for hope and living proof of the gospel to transform lives, one need look no farther than JON LINEBERGER! I've loved this family for decades and prayerfully watched this young man's journey. Today I share his every victory as though it were my own. This is the real life story of the new beginning that is available to any and all of us. Read it and reap!

Dr. O.S. Hawkins
President and CEO, GuideStone Financial Resources

I have heard it said that in order to help someone who is bleeding, you must be willing to hemorrhage yourself. For when you bleed, you give a life transfusion to others! And that is exactly what JON LINEBERGER has done for us in his book. So find your favorite resting place, get yourself your favorite drink and consume this book! Or more appropriately, let it "consume you!" And when all is said and done, you will give praise and glory to God for a life that has experienced "Amazing Grace" and a life that has shared His Grace with US!

So, READ this book and then quickly pass it on to someone who needs this same kind of "Amazing Grace!"

Dr. Dennis Swanberg
America's Minister of Encouragement
Author of TheManCode.net

Anyone reading Jon's story can relate to at least one of his struggles through life. This book demonstrates the truth of Matthew 23:11-12, "But the greatest among you shall be your servant. Whoever exalts himself shall be humbled; and whoever humbles himself shall be exalted." Jon's story is a testament to the truth of the Gospel of Christ. Christ has renewed, Christ has redeemed, and ultimately Christ will receive the glory for a life well lived.

Jason Hoyt
Executive Director
Beta Upsilon Chi, Inc.

What God Did With a Mess Like Me

17 Truths to a Changed Life

Jon Lineberger

Intersect Press
Dallas, Texas

Unless otherwise noted all Scripture quotations used in this book are taken from the Holy Bible: New International Version (NIV), © 1973, 1978, 1984 by International Bible Society, used by permission of Zondervan Publishing House, all rights reserved. Other Scripture references are from the following sources: English Standard Version (ESV), © 2001, by Crossway Bibles, used by permission of Good News Publishers, all rights reserved; The New King James Version (NKJV), © 1982, Thomas Nelson, Inc., used by permission, all rights reserved; The Message, © 2002, NavPress Publishing Group, used by permission, all rights reserved. International Standard Version (ISV), © 2011, Davidson Press, used by permission, all rights reserved. New Living Translation (NLT), © 2009, used by permission Cambridge University Press, all rights reserved. New International Reader's Version (NIRV), © 1996, 1998 by Biblica, used by permission, all rights reserved.

ISBN-13:
978-1469977263

ISBN-10:
1469977265

Printed in the United States of America
2012
Intersect Press
Dallas, Texas

Cover design and interior by Style Publishing Group
Frisco, Texas

www.jonlineberger.com

For information regarding special bulk rate purchases or to schedule Jon for speaking engagements, please email info@jonlineberger.com.

Dedication

To my parents: Dr. Rick and Tracey Lineberger
Thank you for always praying for me, encouraging me, and believing in me.

To my wife: Gina
Thank you for marrying me, for supporting me, and for unconditionally loving me—faults and all. Thank you for believing in the mission God has for my life and allowing me to share the stories in this book.

To my kids: Hailey, Lauren, and Luke
I love you all very much. I hope this book does not embarrass you because the last thing I would want to do is hurt you. Unfortunately, I made some bad decisions in the past, but thankfully and fortunately I was given an opportunity from Jesus Christ to change my life. Hopefully, I have many more years on earth to spend with you, but since I don't know how much time I have left, I believe God wants me to share how He worked in my life so that others may have hope and faith in Jesus Christ. I pray that you will not make the same mistakes I did growing up. Always trust Jesus and think positively. Keep the end in focus. Live for Christ and your life will count.

To: Dr. Gary Cook, President, Dallas Baptist University
Thank you for giving me an opportunity to work at Dallas Baptist University and for your commitment to Christ-centered education.

Contents

INTRODUCTION

The Start of a Long Journey

This book is about how big God is and what He alone can do with a life. It's about the redemptive power of a gracious and loving God who changed my life. I was hopeless and sometimes wanted to give up, but when I submitted to God I found salvation for this life and the life to come.

Much of what I share in this book is difficult for me because doing so makes me feel very vulnerable, and my flesh tells me not to be so honestly revealing. Being so open could cause people to look at me differently. Sharing the stories of my past could hurt my reputation. Being so honest could hinder my chances for future employment. Telling the whole truth could embarrass others. My sincerity could be misjudged. My authenticity could be called into question. My motives could be suspect.

I've prayed and asked God about what to include and what to leave out. As I was writing, I was reminded of John the Baptist's comment when referring to Christ, "He must become greater, I must become less" (John 3:3).

Being transparent and allowing others to see my past is not an easy thing for me to do, but I want to be real and authentic with you. It is embarrassing and humbling for me to openly share my past with the frankness and candor you will see in the following pages. Perhaps some of my reason for writing this book is cathartic; I have benefited from the reflection involved in writing it, but I want this story to glorify God and bring readers encouragement, comfort, and hope in believing that God can change and work in their life.

I have had opportunities to publicly share my testimony and when I'm done, I often want to hide because I'm so ashamed of the person I used to be. At the same time, I don't want to pretend that my life was different and then diminish the extent of the work God has done in my life. I feel obligated out of gratitude to my Savior to share with you how God saved me, changed me, and continues to mold my life. God has richly blessed my life. I want to shout out loud how God has worked in me. I have been given an enormous gift of regeneration, and I feel I must give back.

God's grace to me was and is overwhelming. I believe God wants me to share with others what I have gone through and how He saved me from my desperation. He wants me to show how His grace gave me the courage to climb out of my own hopeless situation into a life of joy and success.

In Acts 20:24 Paul said, "However, I consider my life worth nothing to me, if only I may finish the race and complete the task the LORD Jesus has given me - the task of testifying to the gospel of God's grace."

I am not proud of the stories I will share. I was very much like the prodigal son who wasted much of his life in "riotous living." Please understand that while sharing the truth of my past, I'm not trying to brag or glorify the sin I committed. I am ashamed of what I did.

I share my sin, but I also share the end of the story. Also like the prodigal son, when I finally came home I experienced God's amazing grace. I experienced hope and salvation. I have been through a lot and I openly expose much of what I've experienced so you can see how the power of God has worked in my life to bring about change. You can also possess hope in whatever situation you find yourself because of Jesus Christ.

I've been at the bottom of life and literally wanted to die, even praying for God to take my life. A poor student struggling with ADHD (Attention Deficit Hyperactivity Disorder) and terrible study habits, I was a depressed teenager without much hope. A wild youth who never thought beyond the next fun-filled event, I lacked focus and drive, and I never considered the consequences of what I was doing. I felt I was a disappointment to myself, my teachers, my parents, and God, but He turned each of these around and brought hope and redemption to each situation.

For those who have made some horrible decisions and feel they can never recover from them, there is hope. There is also hope for your loved ones who have gone astray. My encouragement in this book is: Don't give up on them. Keep praying for them and be the example you need to be.

It's not people of the world who will be giving me opportunities or taking away my positions. I live in full assurance that everything I have is from the LORD, and I trust that He is directing and guiding me. I don't have to worry about how my "brand" will be affected if I live to honor and glorify Him. So I am convinced that I must share my experience with others.

What I Now Can See

I'm not a great preacher, and many of you reading this book may know more about the Bible than I do, but as I write this I am reminded of the story in John Chapter 9 about the man born blind. He was a beggar in the streets, and one day Jesus gave him sight. When the Pharisees found out about this they harassed the man demanding, "Who healed you?" Some Pharisees didn't believe it was the same man. Then the man replied, all I know is that I once was blind, but He healed me and now I see.

I will never fully understand Jesus, but what I do know is that He has touched me and now I can see. That is the message I can say to you with confidence. I don't see myself as a major spiritual figure or as a man with authority over other believers, but as a person who has been changed by the power of Jesus Christ. I'm not the same person I use to be. By all means I am not perfect, and as long as I am on earth I never will be. I have my flaws and I've made a lot of mistakes as a Christian. Some of the mistakes I made I knew better than to do, but I still put myself in bad situations. Every day is a maturing process for me. Each day I must ask God to change me. I'm not promised it will be easy, but I must follow where I believe God is leading me.

All throughout the Bible there are stories of lives that have been dramatically changed by God. Maybe you have read most of those stories, but still wonder if God changes lives today. The best way I know how to express to you that God still changes lives is to tell you of my own experience. Much of what I say is difficult for me to relive, but I share it with you so that you may have faith in Jesus Christ and be encouraged. By sharing my experiences, my hope is that someone may be encouraged and his or her life might be changed.

The message I hope that you take away from this book is that no matter what you have gone through, or may be experiencing right now, God can work in your life. He can change you and your situation if you will commit your life completely to Him. I've included some of the low points in my life before I began living for God and some of the high points I've experienced after committing my life to Jesus. All throughout the story you'll see keys that you can implement and follow to help drive a change in your own life. They are refined into the seventeen truths that lead to change.

When I stand before my Savior to give an account for my life, I want to hear Him say, "Well done, good and faithful servant." I hope this story of how God rescued, redeemed, restored and renewed my life will be an encouragement to you. My prayer is that you will be inspired to ask God to work in your own life and allow Him to do so by being obedient to Him so that you can experience the power of God's Amazing Grace.

PART ONE

WHO I WAS

CHAPTER ONE

The Early Years

I was born in Arkadephia, Arkansas to two college students at Ouachita Baptist University. My parents, Rick and Tracey, were married, but I came as a surprise to them. My father played on the football team and was a business major. He originally never intended to enroll at Ouachita. His three older brothers had played football at the University of Arkansas and he had hoped to also play there. My father's hard work ethic and love for football started at an early age. As a young boy he spent his summers at the University of Arkansas pulling weeds from the university's football field for a summer job. He even slept in the dorms at night. One of his high school teammates recently told me that my dad would get the lineman on his high school team in trouble because, as the quarterback, he could out-bench press and out-squat them.

In his senior year of high school he was offered a scholarship to play football at the University of Arkansas, but after summer training he was called in by the coach and told they had given out one too many scholarships and they no longer had a scholarship for him. Not only was his dream of playing football at the University of Arkansas crushed, but my father grew up very poor living in project housing and without a scholarship he would not be able to attend college. Devastated and depressed, he loaded up his stuff and headed back home. At that point he could have given up on his dream of going to college and playing college football, but on his way home he drove past an exit for Ouachita Baptist University. He pulled his car off the interstate and drove up to the campus. He went in, talked with the coach and was offered a scholarship to attend Ouachita and play football.

While not being able to play football at the University of Arkansas was a big disappointment in my father's life, God used that event to build character and direct my dad to attend Ouachita where he received a Christian education. It was at Ouachita that my father decided to surrender his life to the gospel of Christ and become a pastor.

After marrying my mom, who was the college homecoming queen, my dad pastored a few small churches in Arkansas while he was still in college and immediately following graduation. A little over a year after getting married my parents were surprised to discover my mom was pregnant with me, as I was not planned.

When I was a toddler my mother would drop me off in the church nursery before attending the service. My mother told me that she would sometimes get pulled out of the service to get me because I was beating up the other kids in childcare. About two-and-a-half years after I entered the world, my sister Ashlee was born.

When I was three we moved to Fort Worth, Texas for my dad to attend seminary. The first place we lived in was an apartment complex. My dad got a job there to help pay for seminary and living expenses. I made friends with a little girl upstairs, and we would put on our Underoos and play super heroes. She was Wonder Woman and I was Superman. Not long after we moved in, an older man living in the apartments molested me. Unfortunately, this is one of my earliest memories.

I'm sure my parents wondered why this happened to their son. I'm sure their conversations with God went something like, "God, why did you allow this to happen to our boy? We are trying to serve you and do your will and you allowed this to happen. Why does our family have to suffer through this?" The question "Why do bad things happen to good people?" may never be completely answered, but I do know that my family has been through a lot over the years, and we experienced our share of tough times.

Some of the hardships I brought personally upon our family. Some of the difficult situations we didn't ask for or do anything to bring upon ourselves. Through them all however, I watched my father remain steady and consistent, never losing his faith in God nor his love for Him. As the leader of our household, my father guided us through some difficult days and as a result strength, character and a deep-rooted faith in God developed in us all. This strong faith didn't happen overnight, but over many years and through some difficult situations.

An Answered Prayer

Soon after the incident we moved into a triplex closer to the seminary's campus. It is there that I have my first memory of an answered prayer. I wanted a playmate. My mother and I were sitting on the front porch, and we prayed for a friend for me. Immediately after we finished our prayer we opened our eyes, raised our heads, and saw walking toward us a little boy about my age with his mother.

My mom was always willing to pray with me. While I was growing up she read me stories in the Bible as well as books about missionaries who faced various trials and persecutions. I listened to how God protected them. By reading those stories of faith and God to me, she was laying the building blocks for a foundation on which I would, years later, build a strong belief in God. At a very early age I learned what faith in Christ could produce.

As a youngster I had a pretty good life. I loved playing Legos, G.I. Joe, and all kinds of sports. On any given day I might have ridden on dirt bike trails, skateboarded up and down the street and played football, basketball, and baseball with my neighborhood friends all before dinner. Life wasn't always bad, but the good times seemed to be overshadowed by my bad behavior.

To add to it all, I never really liked myself. I didn't think I was normal. My hands and feet were always sweaty, and it was very embarrassing to shake hands with someone or hold hands with a girl. I was always wishing I were someone else, always wondering what it would be like to grow up "normal." I felt different from all my friends. By the second grade, I felt I wasn't as smart as and maybe even a little inferior to my peers, and I wanted to be like everyone else. I think this desperate desire to fit in contributed to some of my rebellious behavior and stunts I pulled to get attention and let everyone else know I was cool.

When I think back over my years between kindergarten and my first couple of years in college the feeling of being in trouble always haunts me. My early "crimes" consisted of things like throwing water balloons onto fast-moving cars from several stories up. One day my friend's mom saw us doing this and told us to stop so we filled up Ziploc sandwich bags with water and threw them instead. We thought we outsmarted his mom, but we should have listened to her. I ended up breaking a windshield of a moving car and was caught. My dad, who was working on a doctorate degree at Golden Gate Baptist Theological Seminary in California, had flown out that morning to attend class. Before he left he told me, as he often did, "Jon, don't get in trouble while I'm gone." That evening I hated to call my dad and tell him that he would have to buy someone a new windshield.

Bad Behavior: The Trend Continues

Resting on Sunday was a rule at our house. One Sunday my dad left early for a meeting before the evening service. As he left he told me to stay inside and rest. After he left, however, I went out in the front yard and teed up some golf balls and started hitting them down the street as I had done on previous occasions. We lived in a residential neighborhood so the golf balls would eventually hit homes. Amazingly, I never broke a window. On this particular occasion a neighborhood friend came over, and I thought I would teach him how to play golf. As I bent down to tee a ball up for him he swung and hit me in the back of the head. Blood was all over my clothes when I went up to the door to tell my mom. She called a neighbor down the street and he rushed us to the hospital. I ended up with stitches.

On another occasion I got in a ketchup packet throwing fight with a friend in the bathroom at church. That didn't go over so well. When my dad found out I was involved in the ketchup fight I ended up cleaning the bathroom floor with a toothbrush.

There was also the time I was at church camp and decided to break the keys on the piano in the chapel. Now why in the world would I do something like that? It was almost as if I couldn't control my impulses. I just didn't think before acting. It was usually after I did something that I thought, "Oh, that might not have been such a good idea." By then it was usually too late. You can imagine how upset my father was when he received a bill for the damages.

Making the Grade in Grade School

My mother decided to homeschool me in first grade and then, from second to fourth grade, I attended a private Christian school. I was really behind the other students when I started private school in second grade. I looked at assignments not knowing what to do. I cried a lot during class because I didn't know how to complete some of the work assigned in class, and I was frustrated. I was such a distraction to the other students that my teacher put my desk against the back wall, away from the other students. This was humiliating and made me feel different from the rest of my classmates. I was later put in a special reading group at school to help me learn to read. My parents also bought me a phonics program on tape that I could listen to and follow along in a book. This program helped me, and I began to catch up with the rest of the class. However, I wasn't always disciplined enough to keep up with it.

Still, by the third grade, I really began to feel accepted by my peers. My teacher, Mrs. Mason, took her time helping me, and I made some great advances in school. At the end of the year I received the Most Improved award. I still have this trophy; it sits on a shelf in my home office.

By the fourth grade, I felt I was one of the smarter kids in class. I had worked hard to catch up and much of that can be attributed to the caring teachers that took time to work with me. The environment was also caring, and we studied and memorized passages from the Bible in class.

I pretty much stayed out of trouble when I was in private school. For the most part, all the students seemed to want to do the right thing. Both the teachers and the students were good influences. I did receive a few licks though. Back then the teachers all had a paddle in their rooms and could apply corporal punishment when they thought necessary. On one occasion I got in trouble for spitting on the ground outside. My teacher warned me on several occasions not to spit, but it was a habit hard to break. I was born in Arkansas. For the boys in that part of the country, spitting is a rite of passage and a part of being a male. As punishment, my teacher made me write, "I will not spit" 200 times.

My sister and I had a lot of friends at church that attended the public school in our neighborhood. Even though we did well in private school, we always felt like the weird kids because we didn't attend school with our friends at church and in our neighborhood. Before my fifth-grade year, my sister and I begged our parents to allow us to enroll at the public school where our friends attended classes. Regrettably, Ashlee and I were successful in influencing our parents to let us change schools. The regrets were mine, not my sister's. A great kid, my sister was a straight "A" student throughout school, and eager to please authority, especially my parents.

During my first year there I quickly started to fall behind. Among other things, I learned to cuss with the best of them. In hindsight, I wish I had remained at the private school where I received a lot more personal attention, studied the Bible, and was influenced to live a Christian lifestyle.

That same year I discovered that girls liked me. This was a new phenomenon because girls at the private school wouldn't give me the time of day. In second grade, a girl at the private school broke my heart. At the end of the school day, we [the students] were all on our way out of class and I handed this particular girl a love note. She took it, rolled her eyes, and threw it, right in front of me, in the trash without reading it. Things were different at the public school. Girls actually gave me the time of day.

By sixth grade I continued to fall further behind. I was never a good reader, and I always hated reading in front of the class. My hands would sweat, and I would be scared to death hoping the teacher wouldn't call on me. I was embarrassed when the other kids heard me struggle. That year I cheated on a book report and was caught. I didn't even cheat very well. I just copied word for word the book's synopsis printed on the back of the book. The teacher asked to see my book and then called my parents.

I was so frustrated in public school because I didn't seem to catch on as quickly as the other kids. I didn't get the personal attention that I had received at the private school. At the public school the lectures weren't enough for me to understand the material, and the classes seemed too fast-paced for me. Most of the time I was daydreaming anyway. I had a very tough time concentrating. I could hear everything going on around me. If someone breathed heavily, tapped a pencil, or made some other noise, it distracted me from what the teacher was saying. It seemed as if I were in a war with all the noises around me, battling for my attention. When I was able to concentrate and pay attention, I felt like I was the only one with questions so I avoided asking any because I didn't want to appear dumb. That is when I started copying my friends' homework. I didn't seem to catch onto things as fast as some of the other students. Once you get behind its hard to ever catch up. No one is going to wait on you everyday so you just get further behind. I thought I had good street smarts, but when it came to book smarts I struggled.

My dating life wasn't suffering though. I had pretty much "gone with," as we use to say, and re-gone with all the pretty girls in my class by sixth grade. Halfway through the year I had written on the front of my notebook, "All My Exes Live In Texas" and listed, by name, all the girls I had "gone with" in my short time at the public school.

Teenage Trials and Errors

In seventh grade, I moved into junior high and began to spend a lot of time in after-school detention. Many times my mom would arrive after school to pick me up and would end up waiting for about 30 minutes only to be told by one of my friends that I was in detention. She never waited and I don't blame her. I walked home from school many a day that year.

I also had to clean up the lunchroom for two weeks because of profanities I yelled out loud in art class. I didn't think about what I was saying. The words came to me, so I said them.

That same year I also learned the "no pass, no play" rule the hard way due to failing a class. I had to sit out of basketball, which was one of my favorite sports. Before I received my grade report, I promised my dad that I would pass all my classes and he purchased me my first pair of Air Jordan basketball shoes. I was so embarrassed when I discovered that all my friends would be playing basketball, and I wouldn't be able to join them. I was even more upset that I had disappointed my dad. I didn't always try or want to do the wrong thing. I just didn't always try to do the right thing.

During that year my seventh-grade boys' Sunday school class held a discipleship weekend. We spent the night at a friend's home. Guess who brought and provided cigarettes to all the guys that weekend? Jon, the preacher's kid, of course. We thought we could get away with smoking the cigarettes if we went outside and smoked them on the side of the house. As you might suspect, the act didn't go unnoticed.

At the end of my seventh grade year my father took a pastorate at another church, and we moved to another city. This was difficult for me because I was leaving all my friends plus my girlfriend who I dated for nine months. That summer I spent mostly by myself. We rented a home while we built another, and I didn't know any kids in our temporary neighborhood. It was a pretty depressing summer. My girlfriend broke up with me after the move because she thought we would be too far apart. I was very hurt. I felt a huge sense of rejection and I was lonely. Even though we were only in seventh grade, the relationship had developed into a physical one. While we didn't have sex the physical touching we did do took our relationship to another level. Becoming physical in a relationship deepened our emotional connection and heightened the level of loss and depression I felt. I was much too immature to deal with those kinds of feelings, and so I spent a lot of time in my room hurt and crying because I missed my girlfriend and many of the friends I had left.

During my eighth-grade year I was diagnosed with ADHD. While it gave me a little relief to get a diagnosis other than being stupid, I still didn't think of myself as being smart. Now it was confirmed that there was something wrong with me and that I was different from everyone else. As a result of the ADHD diagnosis, I was approved for the Content Mastery program available in Texas public schools. This gave me the chance to leave class and receive additional one-on-one attention and help from teacher aides in a semi-private room. I'm not sure this helped me. I wasn't interested in focusing anyway, and I never got much done in the room assigned for Content Mastery students. I usually goofed around with the other students approved for the Content Mastery program.

My eighth-grade year was really tough. As the new guy, I got picked on by some of the "cool" guys. Before we moved I was one of the popular kids in school and could have dated any girl I wanted. As the new kid at a much smaller school I felt very alone. I felt insecure, and I didn't have the comfort of being in the popular crowd like I did before. Additionally, not doing well in school made me an easy target for other people's jokes. That year the girls that I was attracted to didn't return my attention, and I experienced rejection again.

My father told me that when we moved I would get a fresh start. I wanted to be good and stay out of trouble, but being good didn't seem to win me any cool friends or make me popular. When I tried to be good and do what was right, kids made fun of me. One day at lunch, early in the school year, I sat with a bunch of girls. They were talking about one girl losing her virginity. I made a comment about saving virginity for marriage and several of the girls laughed and gave me weird looks. At that moment I felt alienated. I wanted badly to fit in and for people to like me. I didn't want to feel different from everyone else. However, when I tried to be cool and fit in I found myself once again doing things that I shouldn't be doing. While part of me felt guilty for doing the things I knew were wrong, another part of me didn't care because I was getting attention from my peers.

For instance, one day in reading class my teacher saw a pencil fly across the classroom, but didn't know who did it. She scolded the class and warned us not to throw anything else. She left the room for a moment, and I saw my chance to toss another pencil across the room. As the pencil left my fingers the teacher, who happened to be a member of the church my dad pastored, walked back in. It was as if everything suddenly turned into slow motion. She watched as the pencil left my hand, and I couldn't stop it or redirect its flight pattern. The pencil flew right in front of her face, nearly hitting her. The rest of the year I sat in the front of the classroom, facing the wall next to the teacher's desk.

On another occasion a friend and I got passes to go to the restroom. I was always bored in class and would often take a restroom break. I'm not sure how long we were gone, but our teachers eventually came looking for us and caught us gambling on the floor in the restroom. For whatever reason, the teachers didn't punish us.

As the year went on, I continued to struggle in class and as I fell behind in school I became frustrated and continued to fall further behind. I felt like I was caught in a cycle, and I didn't know how to get out of it. It is very humbling when others make fun of you because you do poorly in school. I began to believe that I wasn't smart at all, and I felt inferior to other people.

Words are very powerful. When you begin to listen to people's words and believe them, those words, if negative, can cause a lot of harm by affecting your personality, outlook on life, and sense of self-worth. Sometimes the words of peers, especially for young people, can be more influential and powerful than the words of family members.

Everyone wants to feel like they belong and that they are accepted. Rejection is a powerful and painful force that can crush the spirit. You'd think that as a result of being rejected by people's cruel words that I would refrain from making fun of others at their own expense. However, when you're immature or have low self-esteem you sometimes make fun of others because you believe it will make you feel better or elevate yourself above them. On the contrary, it does quite the opposite. It brings you down and hurts others. To this day I feel terrible and sorry when I think about the people I caused pain with my destructive words and by making fun of them. Whether you are conscious of it or not, the words you say, the looks you give, the acknowledgements shown or lack thereof can affect other people's lives in a dramatic way. Make an effort to show a sincere interest in the life of people you interact with on a daily basis. You have the power to make a difference in someone's life.

> **Be mindful of the influence you have to make others feel accepted or rejected.**

Your Parents Know a Lot

As an adolescent I lived up to the "preacher's kid" reputation: I was rebellious and wanted to do things my way. I thought my parents wanted to keep me from having fun. I didn't understand why I couldn't do many of the things my friends' parents allowed them to do. Looking back I can now see it wasn't that my parents didn't want me to have any fun; they were just older and wiser. They wanted to keep me from getting hurt and out of trouble. Even though it may not seem like it sometimes your parents are looking out for your best interest.

> **Listen to the wisdom of
> your parents.**

Excuses, Excuses

When I was young my bad decisions were more a result of not fully thinking through the thought before acting on an idea rather than outright malicious acts. I have tried to analyze myself and figure out why I made such poor decisions and came to the conclusion that it was probably a combination of factors. I could say I felt too much pressure from the church as a preacher's kid. (By the way, be nice to your pastor and his family. Many times they have a lot of unrealistic expectations to live up to. They need your love, support, and prayers.) I could try to blame my mother for being strict with me or claim that my Native American genes gave me a predisposition toward an addictive personality, or that I had ADHD. But ultimately I alone am responsible for the decisions I made and actions I took. I alone will be held accountable for them.

Think about the choices you make. They will determine who you are and who you will become.

> **You are the sum of your
> choices.**

Chapter Two

Bad Influences

During my freshman year in high school I still struggled academically. I was forced to take remedial courses in math, English, and science. During that year some of my peers began to make fun of me and call me stupid. Some students even began a rumor that I was dyslexic, and I would laugh along with them. Even though I wasn't dyslexic, I would allow others to think I was because it gave me an excuse. This joking bruised my self-esteem; it's no fun being the butt of dumb guy jokes. Throughout high school I never really developed as a reader and continued to struggle.

During my freshman year I also had my first experience with alcohol while hanging out with some friends. I discovered that when I drank I felt more confident and accepted by others. It wasn't always that I wanted to do bad things, but it was the influence of the people that I placed around me.

Birds of a Feather Flock Together

Growing up in church and in a Christian family, I was familiar with many Scripture passages like 1 Corinthians 15:33 which says, "Do not be mislead: Bad company corrupts good character." (The International Standard Version of the same verse says, "Stop being deceived: Wicked friends lead to evil ends.") However, like many other lessons I was taught growing up, this warning didn't sink in immediately.

I can't tell you how true that verse is. It's impossible to hang around someone and not be influenced by them in some way or form, whether good or bad. I wish I would have paid better attention to this principle, but I did not heed its warning.

> **You will become like the people you hang around.**

Don't get me wrong. I was no saint myself; in many cases I was the bad company. Not all my friends in high school were troublemakers and my parents didn't disapprove of all the girls I dated. I did have a few friends that stayed out of trouble. They knew what kinds of activities to not involve themselves in. I wish I had spent more time around these good people. It's possible they could have helped to elevate me, and I wouldn't have gotten in as much trouble as I did. At the time, however, it seemed like more fun to run around with the bad crowd.

I should have remembered that, back in the third grade, when I was attending private school, I received a paddling I felt I didn't earn. When I told the teacher, "But I didn't do it" her response was, "Well, you were standing by the person who did." I should have learned then that the people you hang around will either keep you out of trouble or get you deep in it. My dad use to tell me, "You can't play with something without getting it on you." I wish I would have heeded these lessons, but they didn't sink in for me.

> **Count the cost. All actions
> have consequences.**

More Bad Company, More Trouble

Misbehaving always cost me something. When I was younger the consequences were small, but as I got older the trouble I got into became more serious. During my freshman year I had several encounters with police and security officers for a variety of things.

Toward the end of my freshman year I went to the mall with some friends who decided to shoplift. We all ended up being caught by mall security and even though I personally didn't take anything I was detained along with them. I was guilty by association. When my dad came to pick me up I could see the disappointment on his face and he didn't have to say a word. I never wanted to hurt my dad, I just didn't think through the consequences. Besides, all my friends were doing it and that seemed to make the behavior all right.

Many of the stunts I was involved in I thought were simply boys being mischievousness. Roofing homes was my summer job throughout high school. We would sometimes drive an older vehicle, a Mercury Monarch, to and from job sites and discovered that if you turned off the car while driving and then quickly turned the ignition back on the car would backfire. The sound was so loud it fired out like a shotgun blast. We kept a silver-colored toy gun with us and would drive through neighborhoods pointing the gun at people and backfiring the car. Then we would drive off laughing at their reactions. Some of the people we targeted dropped what they were carrying and dove behind objects.

On one day during the summer before my sophomore year, we were driving down the highway on our way home after a hard day of roofing. We were up to our typical shenanigans when all of a sudden we were surrounded by six police cars and forced to pull over our vehicle. After we did, the police told us to crawl out through the windows. Handguns and rifles were pointed at us from multiple directions. The highway was shut off as we were instructed to lay face down on the highway with our hands behind our heads. The police found the toy gun and we explained ourselves to them, but we were still taken down to the station and charged with brandishing of a weapon facsimile. My father once again went down to the police station to pick me up. I was later assigned a court date and had to appear before a judge. I was placed on probation.

Ironic, Isn't It?

Many of the guys I hung around and got in trouble with I also invited to attend church with me. My youth minister at the time said that I brought more friends to church than anyone else in the youth group. I knew my parents were going to make me go to church whether I wanted to or not, so I thought I could make going more enjoyable by bringing my friends along. Some of the friends I brought made decisions to accept Jesus as their savior. I myself had some emotional experiences and wanted live a better life. Sometimes during high school I made commitments to start over and live a Christian life, but I was not strong enough to resist when confronted by temptations. I also never made Jesus the LORD of my life. I wanted to be a Christian, but I didn't want to give up some of the things I was doing. I wasn't ready to stop living for myself or for my own pleasure.

During that same summer I went on a church youth trip to a theme park out of town. While there I decided to shoplift some items despite the fact that they weren't things I needed or wanted. I don't know why I took them. I guess it was to see if I could get away with it, like stealing was a game. I was caught and detained by two security officers who tracked down my youth minister to come get me. Even now I'm not allowed to return to that park. All of the youth on the trip found out about the incident, and it spread through the church. It was a pretty embarrassing time for my family and me.

Yet, in my sophomore year, because I received more attention from girls, I felt more accepted. I began dating girls my parents didn't approve of and I became sexually active. That choice, because of what was going to happen, still affects me.

I received my driver's license early in the school year. This provided me with a lot more freedom, but it also began a long line of speeding tickets. During my high school years I spent a lot of time working community service hours with the city and listening to defensive driving instructors in order to keep traffic tickets off my record. I wish I had all of the money I spent on traffic tickets when I was a teen in my retirement account today.

My dad gave me a gas card when I began driving to use whenever I needed to fill up the car. However, I wasn't only using the card to fill up the car, but my stomach as well. I bought food as well as beer with it. Also, if I needed cash I would fill up a friend's car with the card and ask him to give me the money. I used my dad's gas card like my own personal ATM card. This episode only lasted until he got the first statement. Then he took the card away from me.

> **Respect and appreciate privileges. They can be taken away easily, especially if abused.**

During football season of my sophomore year I continued to make wrong decisions and began experimenting with marijuana. One evening a friend invited a lot of people to a party at a vacant house he said his parents still owned. Apparently this was not true, and a neighbor called the police. When the police arrived we ran out of the house and tried to escape, but the police ran us all down. I was guilty of trespassing. Once again my dad had to pick me up. The next week the coach suspended me from the homecoming football game for attending this party. I wasn't even allowed to go and watch the game. Throughout the year I continued to make bad decisions.

Then something happened that placed a positive influence in my life. During my junior year Aaron Crawford began attending my church. I was blessed to meet him. His example, that of a sincere Christian, made a difference in my life. Our friendship would eventually play a significant role in helping me move toward turning my life over to Christ.

We were the same age, but he attended a different high school. One Sunday night at church I noticed that he was wearing a fly fishing shirt. Since I enjoyed fishing, I introduced myself to him. We became instant friends and began fishing together. Aaron was a good Christian and had aspirations of being a minister. I enjoyed hanging out with him because I always felt like I was doing the right thing when I did. I should have spent more time with him, but since Aaron and I lived in different cities, I found it easier to hang out with people who weren't living their lives for God.

Not surprisingly, I continued to make bad decisions. One night I went camping with another friend. We had taken a bottle of whiskey and some beer with us. When we ran out of alcohol, we decided to walk to a friend's home nearby. It was in the middle of the night so we didn't knock or ring the doorbell. When we noticed the door was unlocked, we walked right in and went to the liquor cabinet. I can remember getting into a wrestling match with my friend in the living room, and we almost broke a glass top coffee table.

We drank some of the liquor in the cabinet and then found a new bottle of tequila, which we took back to the tent with us. I don't remember anything else that night. The next morning I woke up in the tent with vomit all over my face and in my ear. It was Sunday morning and I said to my friend, "We've got to hurry. We can't miss church." While I might not have been living as a Christian, I knew how to look like one when it came to Sunday. We got to my house as fast as we could, still drunk from the night before. We showered and got cleaned up in time to leave with my mom.

Around the time we arrived at church, the hangover began to sink in. I felt very nauseous and had to leave several times during the service to dry heave in the restroom. After the service I was standing around with a couple of friends when we saw my dad walking toward us. About the same time I felt another dry heave coming and I had to turn around with my back to my dad and dry heaved in the water fountain next to us. I don't think my dad noticed; he didn't say anything to me.

That year my bad grades continued. One day my Spanish teacher said that no one had ever gotten away with cheating in her class. I took that as a challenge. For one particular test students were to stand up in front of the class and give an oral presentation in Spanish. Instead of memorizing my presentation, I wrote it across the top of my brown boots. When it was my turn I stood up in the front of the room, looked down at my boots, and read off the presentation. I didn't get caught, but today I wish I had taken that class more seriously.

If I didn't like a class, I would many times just go down to the nurse's office and take a nap. I did that mostly during geometry class. As a result, I had to take summer school between my junior and senior year in high school to repeat geometry.

> **If you've got to do something you might as well do a good job. If you don't do it right the first time, you may end up doing it again.**

During spring break of my junior year my parents planned a trip to visit the Holy Land in Israel. They left me to stay with our neighbors across the street. After my parents left I was outside mowing the yard when a friend pulled up and said, "Let's go to Padre!" I hadn't planned on it, but the idea sounded good. I put the mower up, grabbed a change of clothes, and we headed down to South Padre Island, Texas, twelve hours away. On the first night there I called my neighbors and told them I was camping a few miles away and that I would be gone a few days. That same night we were unable to get a hotel room or locate our friends so we slept in the car. We had to keep moving from parking spot to parking spot because security guards would walk up, tap on our window, and tell us we couldn't sleep there.

The next day we decided to go into Matamoros, Mexico and party. When we arrived my friends looked at me and said, "Jon, don't get arrested here. If you do you may be here a while." Well, thankfully we did make it out of Mexico, but I guess you could say I am in the U.S. illegally. When we exited Mexico and crossed over the Rio Grande River there was a walking toll bridge. I didn't have any coins with me so I jumped the gate and ran across the bridge into the United States.

When we got back to South Padre that night, I noticed about 20 portable outdoors toilets in a row on the beach. I thought it would be fun to run down the row and push them all over, so that is what I did. All, but one that is. I remember approaching one and hearing someone from inside the portable toilet plead, "Please don't push over this one. I'm in here." I showed mercy to this person.

God really protected me on that trip. It's a wonder that more people don't die or get seriously hurt in South Padre on spring break. Alcohol and drugs were everywhere. People were doing all kinds of careless things. I later learned that my dad had prayed for me every night on his knees while on their trip.

My behavior was often recklessly impulsive. Having ADHD only contributed to my lack of self-control. One warm day that spring, I was at my friend's house, and I thought it would be fun to jump off his second-story roof into the swimming pool. I didn't think about the shallow end being closest to the roof, and when I jumped that's exactly where I landed. When my heels hit the bottom of the pool a jolt went through my body and for a few seconds I thought I was paralyzed. My friend pulled me out and carried me inside. Fortunately, and by the grace of God, I was all right.

But then something truly terrible happened. In the spring of my junior year I discovered that a girl I was dating was pregnant. It was not the healthiest of relationships to begin with. We both lied to, and cheated on, each other often. At only seventeen-years-old, we were both very immature and very scared. I knew that some Christians can be extremely judgmental, and I remember thinking that if the community in which we lived found out I had gotten a girl pregnant my dad might lose his job as a preacher. I thought it would be better to die than for the news to become public.

After agonizing over what we should do, we secretly decided upon an abortion. I knew what I was doing was wrong, but I just wanted the situation to be over. I was much too immature to realize how lasting the effects would be. I found my decision difficult to handle, and I sought out unhealthy ways to cope with my emotions. I think about the choice I made almost every day of my life.

Later that summer my father found a box full of alcohol in my closet. I had stocked the box with beer and various hard liquors so they would be on hand when I needed them. He confronted me about the alcohol and made me take the bottles into the back yard and pour them all out.

My relationship with my family suffered badly over my teenage years, much of it as a result of my poor decisions. My parents couldn't trust me because I lied about a lot of the things I was doing or who I was hanging out with. They knew I didn't use good judgment, if any at all. My mother talked about kids who took drugs, and she asked me if I had ever done them. I of course lied and said, "No," even though I was high at that very minute. My mother was strict and I'm sure as a preacher's wife she felt a lot of pressure to perform at unrealistic levels and present the perfect family. I rebelled against her authority and pretty much wanted to do the opposite of anything she wanted me to do. Our relationship could be described as very strained during this time. And while our relationship had its rocky passages, I know she loved me then and still loves me now.

I knew my parents loved me because I often heard and saw them praying for me. Also my father could not have set a better example. A man's man, he is a loving husband and father, and a devoted follower of Christ. He was authentic, disciplined, and consistent and still is to this day. Basically, he was everything I wasn't. He attended each athletic event I was involved in. Every night he would enter my room and hug me and tell me that he loved me. He did the same for my sister. Some mornings he would leave the house before we were out of bed. He would come into our rooms and kiss us good-bye.

I saw his life behind closed doors and never witnessed him do anything that contradicted his faith. Because of his love for me, it distressed me to see that my actions hurt him. Even though I didn't want to cause my dad pain, I still wanted to live my own life. I wanted to do what I wanted to do, but more than that, I didn't know how to stop my compulsive behaviors.

CHAPTER THREE

The Worst Year of My Life

My senior year of high school should have been one of the best years of my life. Instead, it was the worst. I was starting on both offense and defense on Southlake Carroll's football team. We had won back-to-back Texas state championships the two previous years. Partway through the season, I made some bad decisions at a party and ended up spending a night and day in jail. The head football coach found out about the party, and I was called into his office and kicked off the team.

Devastated, I became very depressed. Since I was a small child, all I ever wanted to do was to play football in college. My father and his brothers had played college football and now I felt like I would not be able to carry on that tradition. I gave up on my dream. I thought no coach, team or college would want me. I had never made plans to go to college because I felt that things would fall into place. I did receive some letters from a few small colleges and thought I would have an opportunity to play at that level, but now that dream seemed far removed.

The suspension also prohibited me from playing basketball, running track, or playing any other sports for the remainder of the school year. Up to this point, my identity was wrapped up in being an athlete. That's where my confidence, value, and self-worth came from. Now that I was not on a team, or performing in the athletic arena, I lost more confidence and self-esteem. I felt like a nobody.

My girlfriend, on whom I had become codependent and emotionally attached to, didn't want to be with me anymore either. That wasn't surprising, since I didn't want her hanging out with her girlfriends or going anywhere without me. Sometimes on Friday and Saturday nights, I would tell her I was coming over to get her, but then go out with my friends and never pick her up. Night after night I would make her stay on the phone with me for hours in an attempt to control her.

I became so depressed that many nights I held a gun to my head. I was angry and hated life, but I couldn't pull the trigger. I didn't want to hurt my dad—he would lose his only son—and I didn't want to go out that way, but I didn't want to live either. I wished I had never been born. I carried so much shame and guilt, and I felt I had made such a mess of my life that there would be no way to recover. I was in so much emotional pain that sometimes I thought I was going crazy. I didn't think there was any hope for me at all.

During this awful time I received the following letter from my friend Aaron Crawford. The letter is dated Sunday, October 2, 1994 and reads:

Dear Jon,

Well you probably know why I am writing you. I am sorry I am not talking to you in person, but I feel I express my feelings better when I write. Anyway, whatever happened, I don't care about what other people say. My heart is broken. Not over what you did or anything like that, but what you are going through now. I know how you feel. Like embarrassed or afraid to show your face. Don't worry I don't blame you! I hold absolutely nothing, totally zero against you. All is forgiven if you are concerned about me. I love you man! You are so special to me, and if you are hurting I want to hurt too. Jon, God is in control of this situation. I know from past experiences. Today I prayed for you continuously. I am not going to desert or abandon you. I am going to be right here to listen, to be your punching bag if you need one, and to be your best friend that will not give up.

Jon, read this passage of Scripture: (please) John 8:1-11 especially John 8:11. If you have asked forgiveness then let go of it. Jesus has lifted this load off of you. Jon, remember I will always be here. If you want to, I do not want you to feel uncomfortable, call me. Don't hesitate call me. You are not in this alone. Lean on me if you want to. My shoulder is here and offered to you. At any time! I will be praying for you! Maybe we can pray together if you want? I would love that! Just like Jonathan and David! I will be your bud.

Forever and always (Just like Wal-Mart) Ha Ha!! Your best friend and bud,

Aaron Crawford
P.S. I'll cry with you if you need to.

I realize today how good a friend Aaron was to me. I should have stuck closer to him, but I was too wrapped up into a destructive lifestyle.

My sister, who was a cheerleader and a good student at my high school, was so embarrassed by me that she transferred to a private school to finish up the year. I wasn't a good brother. Many times I was downright mean to her. To think about how I treated her breaks my heart today. I should have been more of a positive example and influence in her life.

As the year continued I became more depressed. My parents took me to a psychologist, but this didn't seem to help me nor provide me with the fix I was hoping for. During my high school years alcohol and drugs became my way of self-medicating to help me get through life. I used them to cope and deal with my anxieties, insecurities, and emotional stress. In a way it's strange that I tried alcohol or drugs. I've always been a healthy eater and back then I wouldn't even take my ADHD medication because I didn't want it to harm my liver or decrease my appetite. I didn't even drink sodas. To this day I will rarely even take an aspirin. The only way I can explain it is that I was in such mental anguish I was looking for something that would help me escape reality.

It's hard enough growing up and figuring out who you are. On top of that I also held so much shame, fear, hurt, resentment, anger, and pain bottled up inside. The only way I thought I could get through the day and to cope with my emotions was to self-medicate by getting drunk or high. I didn't know how to deal with my struggles so I masked them with alcohol. During lunch breaks at school I would go out to my car and drink. Sometimes I would drink before school.

I was so stressed out, irritated with people and life and frustrated by my struggles in school. I was upset with my relationships and by not being able to participate in sports. I was angry living at home and under someone else's rules. I was frustrated with life, where I was in life, and what I was and wasn't doing.

Ashamed of what I had become, I found it hard to face people and my life unless I was on something to help me escape reality. I felt helpless and powerless to control some of my circumstances. Since I felt like I couldn't control how smart I was, if my girlfriend was faithful to me, or where I lived, I took on a "whatever" mentality. I would have rather faced life inebriated than be forced to deal with the truth. My reputation was worsening and some of my friends did not want me to ride in their vehicles. They would say that I was bad luck, and they thought they would get pulled over by the cops if I rode in their car.

Not a Typical Graduate

In the spring of my senior year I wanted to see if I could stay drunk for 30 days in a row. So I did. I kept beer in my bedroom, under my sink, and in my car. I was also working at a hotel and often had access to alcohol. On one occasion, I went to a suite to set up a bar. I poured myself a few shots and before I knew it, I ended up getting drunk. Thankfully my boss didn't notice.

I could still play the church game really well and thought I was fooling most people, but as I would soon find out I was only fooling myself. One day the assistant principal came and got me out of in-school suspension (for getting into a fight) and asked me to follow him to his office. When I entered his office I saw my parents. He asked me to sit down and began to tell me that I was out of control and that I was going to have to leave the school. Graduation was a month away.

He was right. I was out of control. Sometimes I felt like I was going crazy because my emotions would consume and control me. Tears stung my eyes as I saw the pain on my parents' faces. The assistant principal made a deal with me. He said that if I went to rehab I would be able to walk with the rest of my classmates at graduation. I agreed and left school immediately. I spent the next few weeks in inpatient and outpatient care.

I felt safe in rehab. I didn't have all the outside influences to bring me down and people were constantly encouraging me. I could talk openly about my problems without fear of being judged, but it was not the real world. The days were easy because I was surrounded by a good support system and had very limited choices. There was a night curfew and when I got into bed it was difficult because I was alone with my thoughts. I was a jealous boyfriend and still tormented with thoughts of who my ex-girlfriend might be dating while I was stuck in rehab. I discovered that when you are emotionally attached to someone it's hard to let those thoughts go that preoccupy your mind. But I did make a little progress and began to move past those thoughts.

When the day came for me to leave rehab I had mixed emotions. Part of me was ready to leave and part of me wanted to stay where it was safe and not re-enter reality. It seemed easy to be good in rehab. There was a point system, and if you were really good you got chocolate milk with your meal. When you are locked up in rehab and you aren't able to choose what you get to eat, earning chocolate milk is a big deal.

Around the time of graduation, my church included a special time during a Sunday service to recognize all of the high school graduates who were members of the church. Each graduating senior was given a card to write their name on and the college they would be attending in the fall. The cards were given to a church staff member who, during the service, read the cards. As the staff member read them, names like Baylor, TCU, Texas A&M, and UT Austin were mentioned. On my card I had written that I would be "Going fishing." My mother was so embarrassed when my card was read. She cried all afternoon.

I was able to make my high school graduation ceremony, but since I didn't attend the rehearsal I sat out of order. I was at the end of the line to be called up to receive my diploma. I felt like everyone was looking at me. I had disappeared from school to go to rehab and then showed up at graduation. Even my high school graduation couldn't be "normal" for me.

Chapter Four

A Chance for a Fresh Start

After graduation in May of 1995, I accepted the gracious offer of my Aunt Mary and Uncle Mel to live with them in Texarkana, Texas. I don't think they knew all that was going on in my life. They were building a new home and were going to be out of town a lot that summer. They asked if I would stay at their halfway constructed house and watch over things. The home was huge. I stayed in the completed upstairs of the home while the downstairs was being finished.

I thought this would be an excellent chance for me to escape my troubles and for a while I felt safe. I know now that this was an opportunity from God to get a fresh start, but it didn't take long before I found another drinking crowd. Some of the friends I made were enrolling at a local community college so I thought I would join them. I enrolled, not really knowing what I was doing.

My father also purchased a new truck for me to start off the semester, and I was supposed to help make the payments. One weekend my aunt and I took my truck to visit my cousin who was living in Little Rock. Another one of my cousins was attending college there, and he was a member of a fraternity. I called him up and he invited me to a fraternity party that night. We purchased two bottles of whiskey and got really drunk. I woke up the next morning on a couch in an apartment, not sure how I got there or where I was. I didn't even tell my aunt I would be out all night. I woke up my cousin and told him that we had to hurry back so that we could go to church with my aunt. We made it back just in time to shower and join them for church. My aunt never said a word. Once again I knew how to look like I was doing what was right, especially when I wasn't.

Frustrated and bored, I struggled in college my first semester and skipped quite a few classes. I didn't catch on in the beginning of the semester so nothing made much sense. By the end of the semester I received a 1.17 GPA (Grade Point Average)—a "D-" average—on a 4.0 scale. The only college-level classes that I received credit for were art appreciation and racquetball. I passed art appreciation because I convinced the teacher that raking leaves was landscaping and that landscaping was art. I raked her yard for extra credit. She gave me a "C." I lied to my family about my grade report and told them that I had made better grades than I did. I also didn't do very well at keeping up with my truck payments. Around the same time my aunt found where I had been storing all my hard liquor in my room. She confronted me, but I played it like everything was under control.

A Bad Turn

A couple of weeks after my first semester in college ended, I was still living with my aunt and uncle. I wasn't sure if I would return to school. One of my friends from back home called and said he was headed to Bourbon Street in New Orleans to party for New Year's Eve. I went along with him, and I didn't tell anyone I was leaving. That night I got stupidly drunk on Bourbon Street and found myself separated from my friend. I remember sitting down on a step in a side alley and throwing up. I was close to passing out.

Earlier that night I had walked by some Christians who were handing out salvation tracks. They tried to hand one to me but I didn't take it; yet doing so bothered my conscience and made me feel a little guilty. As I sat on the step being sick and feeling miserable, I felt two people grab my arms and pull me up. I thought for a moment that someone might be robbing me. When I looked up I noticed it was the same people I saw earlier that evening handing out salvation tracks. The man said to me, "We need to get you home." They walked me over to the curb and flagged down a taxicab. When they opened the door to the cab that pulled over I saw my friend sitting in the back seat. It was truly a miracle.

I know now that God was watching out for me that night, not because I am anyone special, but possibly because my parents prayed for me every day and night. I don't know the names of those people who helped me into the taxicab that night; for all I know they could have been angels. Whoever they were I am thankful they were out there being witnesses for Christ. They may have saved my life.

My aunt and uncle were upset and disappointed that I didn't tell them I was going to New Orleans. Not only had I worried them, but my grandmother, who had Alzheimer's disease, went missing from a nearby retirement home that same night, and they needed my help in finding her. Once again I had let down a lot of people. My aunt and uncle had been very good and generous to me.

After that incident, my father told me that if I wasn't going to go to school, and if I was just going to mess around, I needed to move back home. I wasn't interested in going back to school. My grades were always horrible and I thought school wasn't for me. I loaded up my stuff that day and moved back home. I know this upset my aunt, who cried when I left.

When I got home I fell right back into the same old habits and same old crowd. I was drinking a lot, occasionally using drugs, and making truly bad decisions. A girl I dated during this time introduced me to new drugs. One night she laced my joint with cocaine. On another occasion she gave me some pills to take while I was drunk. I didn't know what they were, and I was already much too wasted to notice any effects. I am grateful to God that I never overdosed.

That spring I went to visit one of my friends who attended a college out of town. We partied hard that weekend, using alcohol and taking drugs and going to a strip club. One night my friend mentioned a "massage parlor" in town. On the way out there we drove between 70 and 80 miles and hour on a stretch of highway. I decided that I was going to play stunt man, and I climbed out the window of the truck onto the windshield while speeding down the highway. I then proceeded to climb all over the outside of the fast-moving truck. When I went to get back into the cab through the window I bounced my feet onto the ground and let the momentum carry my legs back and into the truck bed. I thought it was fun, kind of like the Lone Ranger doing stunts on his horse, so I did it several more times.

When we arrived at the massage parlor my friends went in the back room. I stayed out in the waiting area as I didn't want to pay for a "massage." By that time I was so drunk that I passed out on the couch. Fortunately I wasn't robbed and the police never raided the place while I was there.

My destructive lifestyle continued for nine more months. So many times I had gotten so drunk that when I woke up the next day I didn't know where I was or how I got there. Many times I was the driver and responsible for getting others home. All during this time I was on probation and, if arrested, could have served time. I finally got to the point where I was so sick of myself that I began to ask God to take my life. Each night when I went to bed I would hope I wouldn't wake up. Some nights I even prayed that God would not allow me to wake up.

A Turning Point

One night, in the fall of 1996, I prayed for God to give me another chance. While I didn't want my life's story to end at such a low ebb, I wasn't ready to fully give my life over to the LORD. Still, I began to feel a tug and a greater consciousness of the wrong I was doing.

Then New Year's Eve arrived. I purchased a lot of alcohol and was ready to party. This time however, after taking one drink I felt like I couldn't do it anymore. I poured out all the alcohol I bought for the evening.

About two weeks into the new year, I couldn't hold out any longer. I knew that I needed to make a decision to live my life for Christ and to quit giving into my own selfish ways. I'd had enough of that lifestyle. My dad always told me to give Jesus a chance, and I would tell him that I had and it didn't work, but I never really gave Jesus 100%.

Aaron Crawford helped give me the courage to make that decision. I believe God put him in my life because He knew I would go through some difficult times. One weekend Aaron was home from college, and we went driving to go look at some fishing lures at a nearby store. At the time, Aaron was a ministry student at Dallas Baptist University. On the way there I pulled my truck over and told Aaron how I had been struggling with making a decision to give up the things I had been doing and live for Christ. Aaron prayed with me right there.

I told Aaron that I wanted to dedicate my life to Christ. Since the next day was Sunday, he said he would walk down the aisle of the sanctuary with me during the invitation at the end of the worship service. (It's the time when those who want to make a public decision to live for Christ do so.) He asked if I wanted him to accompany me. I did. When my dad gave the invitation and stood ready to greet anyone making a decision, I walked down the aisle, reached out and grabbed him and told him that I wanted to begin living my life for God. I started weeping uncontrollably and couldn't stop. My dad hugged me and told me he loved me. He said, "When you were born we gave you to God."

> **Transformation begins with a committed relationship with Jesus Christ.**

That was the best day of my life. I felt so much relief. I felt like I had been at the bottom of a dog pile and someone came in and started throwing people off. I could finally breathe and exhale. John 8:36 says, "So if the Son sets you free, you shall be free indeed."

I came to God with so much baggage. I carried around so much guilt and shame. I knew at that moment Jesus had come into my life and began peeling away all the shame and guilt I had been living with. I felt like I was finally free from the sin that had been dragging me down. I no longer had to be a slave to sin. I truly felt born again.

This was the fresh start I needed, but it didn't make me perfect. In the past I made so many promises to God that if He would get me out of some mess I had gotten myself into that I would live for Him. I broke those promises so many times. I wanted this time to be different. I knew I would have to stop hanging out with the crowd I was running around with. I knew I needed to leave the girl I was dating. I had tried to make the relationship with her work for a short while, but I kept falling back into the pattern of sin I knew I needed to stop. She was a beautiful sweet girl, but she didn't understand the changes I needed or wanted to make. Since she wasn't ready to make a commitment to live for the LORD, I couldn't expect her to do so. I hoped she would make the same decision for her life, but I couldn't decide for her how she was going to live. I did, however, have to decide how I was going to live. I did have to take ownership for my choices and actions.

> **You are responsible for making your own decisions.**

As a Christian, I realized that my decisions had to be made in light of God's word. Proverbs 13:20 says, "Whoever walks with the wise becomes wise, but the companion of fools suffers harm" (ESV). I knew I needed to put myself around people that also wanted to live for Christ.

Follow the Right Crowd

It's not enough to not hang around the wrong type of people. You must place yourself among people who will be a positive influence in your life. Aligning yourself with the right people will help you move forward in life. Align yourself with the wrong people and you'll move backward. To move ahead you need to strategically manage the voices you allow yourself to listen to by placing yourself around people who will speak truth into your life. Doing so will go a long way in determining who you will become.

> **Put yourself around people you want to be like.**

I wanted to make the right choices and to put myself around people I wanted to be like. However, I knew I wasn't yet strong enough to resist my old vices. I needed the influence of authentic Christians to help me stay out of trouble.

I remember right after I decided to live for Christ I went over to visit a friend who had not yet made the same decision. As soon as I walked in and sat down he handed me a beer. I took one sip and at that moment I knew I needed to leave. I thought of an excuse and left.

It was very difficult for a while because I didn't have very many Christian friends other than Aaron, and he was at school most of the time. All the Christians I knew who were my age I thought were nerds. For a while this made the weekends lonely. I spent a lot of time alone crying out to God and thanking Him for taking away my sin and guilt. I can't explain how grateful to God I felt. It was as if I had been pardoned from a life sentence. I wanted to praise and thank God all the time. My singing voice isn't very good, and I only know a few cords on the guitar, but I would play my guitar and make up praise songs as worship to Him. This time was a tremendous blessing in my life. I was able to develop a deep and meaningful relationship with Jesus Christ that sustains me to this day.

Proverbs 23:17-18 says, "Do not let your heart envy sinners, but always be zealous for the fear of the LORD. There is surely a future hope for you, and your hope will not be cut off."

I clung to this promise and I began to pray that God would surround me with Christian friends that I could relate to and develop friendships with. As I attended church and tried to seek out Christian friendships, it wasn't long before God began to surround me with supportive Christian people. Many of the people I thought were nerds weren't so nerdy after all, and they became big encouragers. A college-age Bible study class at my church started around that time, and I began attending it. The Bible study helped to deepen my worship of God and strengthen my understanding of Him. I was also able to invite some of my friends who didn't attend church to start going with me. One of my invited friends, Zach Poling, made a commitment to Christ and went on to complete a degree at a Christian college and earn a master's degree from a seminary. Zach is now serving as a minister and is currently writing a book.

There is a difference between hanging out with people that are not living their life for God and putting yourself around them to be a witness for Christ. Sometimes it can be a tough and narrow road to navigate, especially for a new believer trying to change and put away old habits, but it can also be difficult for even the most tenured believers. The keys are to remain in close fellowship with Jesus and to measure your progress as a believer by continually asking yourself, "Am I moving forward or backward in my faith in Christ?"

A barometer to measure the type of person you are is by looking at the type of people you attract. John Maxwell, in his book The 21

Irrefutable Laws of Leadership: Follow them and people will follow you, calls this phenomenon the Law of Magnetism. If the type of person attracted to you is not the type of person you want to become, or at least he is not striving to become the same type of person you want to be, some changes in your own life are probably in order.

False Guilt

God used this Bible study, and the people I met through it, to help deepen my walk with Him. But during this same time Satan began to remind me of my past. He tried to bring thoughts in my head of sins I had committed and cause me to feel depressed, defeated, and unworthy. My Christian friends rallied around me, and I told myself again that those feelings were not from God, that my sins had been forgiven, and that this was false guilt. In Romans 8:31-38 Paul tells us that if we are justified in Christ no one can condemn us and that in Him we are more than conquerors. While I came to this realization it still took some time and prayer for me to let go of this guilt. From then on, each time Satan tried to remind me of my past, I reminded him of his future.

When God forgives you and sets you free from sin you are no longer a prisoner to sin. You don't have to live a defeated life.

Being a young man I also wanted to date, and I sought a girl that wanted to live her life for Christ. Since fifth grade I was the type that always had a girlfriend. I rarely went any length of time without one. This time however, I wanted to be very careful in whom I chose. I didn't want to fall back into the type of past relationships I knew so well. I wanted to do things right, but I also needed someone who could understand and accept my past. As I prayed for the right girl, I tried to wait patiently.

Time went by and occasionally I would meet someone and wonder, but then I would receive confirmation that she was not the right person. Then I re-met someone that I knew, but had never really known. We went to the same high school, but were in different grades. She had just graduated from college and moved back home. One Sunday at church we spoke and exchanged phone numbers. I will never forget how excited I was to get her number. I showed it off to my friend Zach, and we slapped high-fives. I began to hang out with this girl as friends for a while and then started "officially" dating after taking her out one Sunday for lunch.

PART TWO
FOLLOWING CHRIST

CHAPTER FIVE

A Rocky Beginning

After becoming a Christian, I thought God was going to bring awesome opportunities my way, and I could sit back and let God do all the work. Well, a year went by and I was still floating through a local community college, passing six or nine credit hours at a time. I still didn't like school and found it difficult to concentrate in class. I thought that school was a game and that I could possibly get by without it.

Nevertheless, I really wanted to be smart and "scholarly." I remember visiting my childhood friend, Eric Herrstrom, when he was a student at Baylor University. (Today he is a minister.) When I visited his apartment in Waco I saw a well-worn desk with a shelf full of books. I remember thinking, "I want to be smart like Eric." That moment was a real inspiration for me.

School was awfully frustrating because I was an extremely slow reader, and I had trouble comprehending what I read. My mind would wonder and daydream, and I also had trouble understanding and comprehending what I was reading. I wasn't sure that I had it in me to be smart or to read like my friend Eric or my father. (My father cataloged his own library and reads at least one book a week.)

Distractions drove me crazy. In college, students would bring food in class or chew gum. I was angry through every class because I had to battle to hear the professor over someone eating chips out of a bag or popping their gum. I wondered if I would ever graduate because I thought there was no way I would ever be able to sit through hundreds of classes while being so distracted. For people with ADHD, sitting in class can seem like listening to a symphony when you only want to hear a piano recital; you hear everything. Every little noise can take one's focus away from the instructor. Besides all of that, I wasn't interested in school and didn't care much about studying or going to class.

At the time I was working at a hotel waiting tables and I had no real plans for a career. I worked as a server in the restaurant, in the banquets department, and in room service, as well as a bellman at the front desk. The hours could sometimes be rough. Depending on what department I worked in, I could have to be at work by 5:00AM or be getting home from work between 12:00 and 2:00AM. The job was good, but I didn't really see much of a future in it. While I worked hard I didn't get a sense that my bosses saw much potential in me, or at least they didn't appear to care to invest in me. I wanted to work behind the front desk at the check-in counter, but I didn't think I was smart enough nor did I have the confidence to ask for the position. I was waiting for my ship to come in without actively pursuing it.

That summer I needed surgery and due to the nature of it my doctor recommended that I not perform any serious heavy weight lifting thereafter. As a weight lifter since seventh grade, I was prideful about my muscular build. Without weight lifting I quickly lost about 30 pounds of muscle, and I began to become insecure about my appearance. I placed a lot of my value in my body and how I looked, and I was known for having a good physique. Now I thought I was again losing more of my value and identity. I enjoyed hearing the girls tell me what a good body I had. I used to think that although I wasn't smart at least my body was good. I thought I was all brawn and little brains and now I didn't even have brawn. That summer I took only three credit hours at a junior college and earned a "D" (a 1.0 GPA) in the course.

To top it off, I wrecked my truck into the back of another vehicle and my insurance company dropped me because of all the accidents I had been involved in. After I got my truck repaired I couldn't make the payments on it so I gave it to my dad to trade it in. He was gracious enough to give me his old Oldsmobile Cutlass Ciera Sport. (I never could figure out what was "sport" about the four-door Oldsmobile, but it was a smooth-riding automobile.) However, now I didn't even have a sweet ride to drive. Instead, I was driving my dad's "old bomb." I thought there was no way I could look cool in that car. It was another humbling experience.

That fall I enrolled in nine credit hours at the junior college and made two "Cs" and a "D" (a 1.66 GPA). At the end of that semester I didn't feel like school was where I needed to be. Hoping I would find a more professional line of work, I didn't enroll for the spring semester. Then, as the spring semester rolled around my girlfriend broke up with me. She was three years older and ambitious, with a good job. I don't think she saw me going anywhere in life and she was ready to make plans. Although I had ambition, I lacked the confidence and know-how to do anything. Our breakup was devastating, and I became very depressed. I thought this was the woman that God had wanted me to marry. Even worse, she started dating someone else. The first night of our breakup, I got drunk. I was still immature and weak in my walk and faith in Jesus Christ. When I faced my first real trial I went back to old habits instead of trusting in and leaning on Christ.

During this time I began to withdraw from friends. I was feeling so hurt. It was too hard for me to go to church and put on a fake smile for others I would see there, especially my ex-girlfriend. I spent a lot of time alone in my bedroom and didn't want to get out of bed in the mornings. Some days I isolated myself, which only made my depression worse. Other days I wanted to be around friends and didn't want to leave them. I couldn't concentrate at work and started calling in sick. I asked my boss to take me off the work schedule for a while. Consumed with the breakup, I wanted desperately for us to get back together. I was a mess. The depression had debilitated me and hindered me from functioning properly. On one occasion I couldn't even walk down the hallway to my bedroom and my dad had to catch me as I fell. My world seemed to be crumbling around me. When I was alone in my car sometimes I would yell and scream, hit my steering wheel and ask God "Why?" I couldn't pull myself together. I couldn't sleep, and I was desperate for rest. Many days I would go up to the church when no one else was there, walk into the sanctuary and lay on a pew. It was the only place I felt at peace and secure, where I could find some relief. I would talk with God until I talked myself to sleep.

Motivational Words
One weekend I stayed with my Aunt Mary and Uncle Mel. My

girlfriend and I had planned to go together to visit them, but that changed after the breakup. I was noticeably upset and broke down about it with my aunt and uncle. They listened and tried to comfort me.

During my stay I noticed a book by Norman Vincent Peale titled A Guide to Confident Living. I normally wouldn't pull a book off a shelf and start reading it, but the title intrigued me, and I was at a point in my life where I needed some confidence. Once I opened the book and started reading I couldn't put it down. I read halfway through the book during that weekend and surprised myself. Up until that point I had only read one book. It was a book, less than 100 pages long, on football. My aunt told me to take the Peale book home and finish it. I even bought a dictionary because I didn't understand all the words.

The information in the book really resonated with me. After a while, I began to gain back some composure. I began to spend a lot of time alone with God. I would wake up early in the morning, grab my fishing rod, put a Christian book and my Bible in my backpack, and walk up to a nearby pond. I would fish a little and read a little, alternating back and forth. I'd find a park bench or picnic table to stretch out on; sometimes I would fall asleep reading.

I looked for more books by Norman Vincent Peale. The next one I read was The Power of Positive Thinking. I prayed that God would give me a desire to read and that He would help me to read faster and to help me understand what I was reading. I wanted to be scholarly like my father and friend Eric.

As I prayed for God to improve my reading ability, I worked earnestly at reading. I've heard that we are to pray as if it all depends on God and work as if it all depends on us. John Bunyan said, "You can do more than pray after you have prayed, but you cannot do more than pray until you have prayed…Pray often, for prayer is a shield to the soul, a sacrifice to God, and a scourge to Satan."

As I worked at reading, God began to give me a hunger and a desire for more. I developed a love for reading. In a little over three months time I read through the entire New Testament and almost a dozen other books.

> **As you pray for something, work toward it, putting your faith to work.**

The more I read, the more wisdom I gained and the more I wanted to be like Christ. Romans 12:2 says, "Do not conform any longer to the pattern of this world, but be transformed by the renewing of your mind. Then you will be able to test and approve what God's will is – his good, pleasing and perfect will."

The more I read the more I wanted to read, and the more my mind was renewed, the more I understood God's will through Scripture. I wanted to soak in as much wisdom as I could. I wanted to steep a long time in God's presence, like a tea bag in hot water.

A Wilderness Experience

Looking back now, I see that God was taking me through a wilderness experience. He was maturing me as a believer and helping me to depend on Him for all my wants and needs. I realized that I was still codependent on a girlfriend for my security instead of on Jesus. Forced to go through these losses and then spending time alone with Jesus, being isolated from the rest of the world helped develop my own authentic faith in Christ. I've heard it said that God does not have any grandchildren; we cannot be saved through our parents' faith. Our parents can help lead us to a faith in Christ and teach us about God, but everyone must come to their own faith in Christ and make their own decision to accept Jesus and become a child of God. Growing up, I learned about Jesus and I witnessed my parent's faith and how God answered their prayers, but I never fully developed my own faith in God.

I realized that until this point I had put too much value and faith in other things besides God. I had been wrapped up in temporal things like into my physical appearance and what I drove. I had invested more time in dating relationships than I had in my relationship with God.

I'm not saying that it's wrong to have a nice car, a good physique, or an attractive girlfriend or boyfriend. What is wrong is placing too much importance in those things or making them our focus, that is, putting other things besides God at the center of our lives. I had focused too much on building up what was on the outside than what was on the inside. I had spent more time working on perfecting my body than working on perfecting my soul. Instead of being egocentric and focused on myself, I needed to become God-centric and place Him at the center of everything I did.

So while I ended up driving my dad's old Oldsmobile for four years, I learned a priceless lesson. I found out that it's not important what you drive. A car does not make you more valuable as a person. People will like you regardless of what you drive and if they don't they aren't worth hanging around in the first place.

Cars get old and dented up. They lose their luster. If you gain confidence from what type of car you drive, what happens when you no longer own a flashy car? The same goes for a toned body or an eye-catching girlfriend. Placing your hope in these things will produce a counterfeit confidence and you may not have them forever. Your relationship with Christ and the security you have in Him will last for eternity.

While at the time I might have been experiencing what seemed to be losses in my life, God used those experiences to mature me and teach me that my value and identity should not be wrapped up in earthly and temporal things, but rather in God. Things of this world can come and go, but the LORD lasts forever, and he will always be there. God will never reject us if we are in Christ. If our confidence is in Him, we will not lose it.

A variation of Matthew 16:25, "For whoever wants to save his life will lose it, but whoever loses his life for me will find it," is mentioned six times throughout the Gospels (Matthew 10:39; Matthew 16:25; Mark 8:35; Luke 17:33, Luke 9:24; John 12:25). I had to lose my life to find it. I had to lose my confidence to find it. I had to die to self, to my own selfish desires and live in Christ to find life. I started to understand that nothing of this world is secure, but if my security, identity, and confidence are in the LORD they will never fade away. While those experiences of loss were painful I am grateful for the lesson I learned; only God can fulfill my needs and desires.

A Confident Turn

I began to pray that God would give me confidence and as I would pray I worked at being confident. I tried to push myself outside my comfort zone and stretch my level of confidence.

I believe that as we ask God for things we should also work toward them. Scripture tells us, "And I will do whatever you ask in my name, so that the Son may bring glory to the Father" (John 14:13). As I began to pray for confidence and also worked to be confident, my confidence level began to increase. My confidence however, was not in myself, but rather in the LORD. I was confident that He could work in me, through me, and use me. My prayers for confidence were being answered and my faith in God was increasing every day.

Ask God for wisdom.

I needed all the help I could get so I also began to pray for wisdom. James 1:5 says, "If any of you lacks wisdom, he should ask God, who gives generously to all without finding fault, and it will be given to him." As I prayed I also began to seek out wisdom by reading and hanging around wise people. As a result of asking God for wisdom and pursuing wisdom I began making better decisions. I would take the time to be wise and think through my decisions. God gave me clearer thinking and I also began to understand Scripture more.

A great example of God giving someone wisdom that asked for it was King Solomon, who is regarded by many as the wisest person to ever walk the earth. The book of 1 Kings shares the story of why Solomon was so wise.

1 Kings 3:5-14
At Gibeon the LORD appeared to Solomon during the night in a dream, and God said, "Ask for whatever you want me to give you." Solomon answered, "You have shown great kindness to your servant, my father David, because he was faithful to you and righteous and upright in heart. You have continued this

great kindness to him and have given him a son to sit on his throne this very day. "Now, LORD my God, you have made your servant king in place of my father David. But I am only a little child and do not know how to carry out my duties. Your servant is here among the people you have chosen, a great people, too numerous to count or number. So give your servant a discerning heart to govern your people and to distinguish between right and wrong. For who is able to govern this great people of yours?" The LORD was pleased that Solomon had asked for this. So God said to him, "Since you have asked for this and not for long life or wealth for yourself, nor have asked for the death of your enemies but for discernment in administering justice, I will do what you have asked. I will give you a wise and discerning heart, so that there will never have been anyone like you, nor will there ever be. Moreover, I will give you what you have not asked for—both wealth and honor—so that in your lifetime you will have no equal among kings. And if you walk in obedience to me and keep my decrees and commands as David your father did, I will give you a long life."

1 Kings 4:29-34
God gave Solomon wisdom and very great insight, and a breadth of understanding as measureless as the sand on the seashore. Solomon's wisdom was greater than the wisdom of all the men of the East, and greater than all the wisdom of Egypt. He was wiser than any other man, including Ethan the Ezrahite—wiser than Heman, Calcol and Darda, the sons of Mahol. And his fame spread to all the surrounding nations. He spoke three thousand proverbs and his songs numbered a thousand and five. He described plant life, from the cedar of Lebanon to the hyssop that grows out of walls. He also taught about animals and birds, reptiles and fish. Men of all nations came to listen to Solomon's wisdom, sent by all the kings of the world, who had heard of his wisdom.

Over the years I have realized more and more that when I am not seeking after God's wisdom my own decisions can fail me. When I trust in God, He never lets me down. My dad's favorite verses from the Bible are Proverbs 3:5-6, "Trust in the LORD with all your heart, and lean not on your own understanding; in all your ways acknowledge Him, and He will direct your paths" (NKJV).

I also prayed that God would help me to be humble. This can be a scary thing to pray for. I knew praying to be humble might mean that I would go through some humbling experiences, yet I wanted to be used by God. I prayed many times for God to use me however He desired, and I was willing to allow God to remove any obstacles in my life that might hinder me from being used by Him.

Chapter Six

My Education Continues

Before the summer of '98, I felt God wanted me to go back to school full-time. I had some money saved up and I thought I would go back to the community college near my aunt and uncle, rent an apartment, find a job, and finish up what I could there. I wanted to be out on my own. God, however, had other plans for me. About a week before I was going to move, I was driving on a stretch of highway, hydroplaned, and spun my Oldsmobile into a concrete guardrail. Amazingly, it was a one-car accident, but I ended up using all the money I had saved to pay for car repairs. I wasn't able to move on as I had planned.

Once again I wasn't sure which direction to go, but I still felt I needed to get back into school. I enrolled at the local community college near my hometown. I realized that God wanted me to give school my best effort. He was not going to give me an "A" in a class or hand me a good-paying job. He wanted me to work hard, and he would reward and bless my hard work. In My Utmost for His Highest Oswald Chambers said, "God will not give us good habits, He will not give us character, He will not make us walk aright. We have to do all that ourselves; we have to work out the salvation God has worked in. If you hesitate when God tells you to do a thing, you endanger your standing in grace."

I enrolled for 10 credit hours that summer at the local community college. Around the same time, a lady in my church took a job out of town but wanted to keep her condominium in the area. She asked me if I would like to stay in her condo for the summer and watch over it. This was a great opportunity for me, and I jumped on it. It was a growing time for me spiritually and for my overall maturity. I had a lot of time alone to study, read, and grow as a Christian. During this time I read my first Shakespeare play, Much Ado About Nothing.

Yet I was still having a hard time dealing with the breakup with my girlfriend. I was trying to discover my worth as a person and wondering what God's plans were for my life. These were puzzles most Christians struggle with. Even though I didn't like to take prescribed drugs, I took an antidepressant for a while because I was so desperate to get some relief.

I knew God loved me, but there were days that I was so depressed that I literally had to make myself get out of bed, look in the mirror and tell myself, "I'm going to have a good day. I'm going to be successful and I'm going to be productive." This was a technique I learned from The Power of Positive Thinking. The process of seeing myself and hearing myself say these words really did give me a small boost, which was enough to help me get ready and out the door. (Peale also encourages readers to personalize Psalm 118:24 and say the verse out loud three times before getting out of bed; "This is the day the LORD has made; 'I' will rejoice and be glad in it.")

The condo I lived in that summer was a long drive away from the community college. On the way to school each morning I would listen to radio broadcasts like Focus on the Family with Dr. James Dobson, In Touch with Dr. Charles Stanley, and Insight for Living with Chuck Swindoll. By the time I arrived at school my mind was focused and my attitude was right. Those radio broadcasts made a huge impact on my life. They fed me with stories, illustrations, and encouragement that God could and would make a difference in my life. I remember praying for God to work in my life the way those ministers said He could, like the way He worked in the life of David as recorded in the Bible.

At the end of the summer term I passed all three courses I was enrolled in. I received two "Bs" and a "C." I was so excited. In the previous three years I accumulated only about 18 transferable college-level hours. Now, in one summer, God helped me complete 10 whole credit hours. I was working hard and praying for God's help and seeing God work in me.

That same summer my dad took me to visit Houston Baptist University (HBU). At the time I didn't know why. I never even heard of the school. But after my visit, I decided that was where God wanted me to attend college. What a blessing that decision turned out to be. I also came to realize why God needed to remove me from my relationship with my girlfriend. If we were still dating I would most likely have never left the Dallas/Fort Worth area or attended HBU, and as a result I would have missed out on a huge blessing.

Moving to Houston was great for me personally. I didn't know anyone at HBU and no one knew me, or my past. Yes, not knowing anyone was a little intimidating at first, but with God's help I was able to start clean and build a whole new reputation for myself. There wasn't anyone there reminding me of the person I used to be or of the horrible things I had done.

While a fresh start was a relief, my time at HBU didn't start off well. My first quarter was tough and I made a 1.33 GPA, another "D" average. I was put on academic probation, and I thought I was going to have to move back home. I thought I would never finish college. I began to question whether school was right for me or if my hope of accomplishing a college degree was even possible.

One day during fall break I said to my mom, "I wish I was as smart as dad." She looked at me and said, "You're smarter than dad." I'm not sure what made her say or think that, or if she really believed it. Maybe she was mad at him that day or possibly she was just trying to encourage me. Whatever her reason was, the comment elevated my perception of my own intelligence a little. What parents say to their kids can have a huge impact on a child's outlook. Words can build them up or tear them down.

At the end of fall break, my dad encouraged me to go back the next quarter and try again. I can remember thinking that if I could just maintain a 2.0 GPA I could graduate. I prayed to God and told Him that I needed His help. I remember thinking that if God could make the blind see, lame walk, and deaf hear, then surely He could change me, too. God could help me graduate from college. I knew that God wanted me to work hard and that the whole reason I was at HBU was to earn an education.

My poor GPA the first quarter was probably a combination of me spending too much time socializing, not having good established study habits, procrastinating, and facing more rigorous academics. I realized that I needed to change my study habits and to take on a new mentality about studying.

I learned a lot from failure—mainly that it stinks. I no longer wanted to be known as the guy who wasn't smart. When I returned to HBU the next quarter I took on a new attitude. I decided that I would do all I could at the beginning of the term to make the best grades. That way, at the end of the term, I wouldn't be scrambling to pass or asking my professor for extra credit to pass. I remember thinking that if I could work on getting good grades at the beginning of the term then I could relax a little at the end of the term.

I believed God wanted me to be successful in school, and I knew I needed His help. One area I needed to work on was my own self-discipline and self-control because these traits pleased God. As 2 Timothy 1:7 says, "For the Spirit God gave us does not make us timid, but gives us power, love and self-discipline."

Work to increase your self-discipline.

As I worked on my self-discipline, I would pray for self-discipline. I believed God would answer my prayers because of 1 John 5:14-15, which says, "This is the confidence we have in approaching God: that if we ask anything according to his will, he hears us. And if we know that he hears us—whatever we ask—we know that we have what we asked of him." It is not God's will that I be timid.

Before studying, I would try my best to find a quiet place with no distractions. I would pray to God and ask Him to help me recall what I was about to study and to bless my hard work. Many times before studying I would read Scripture and some of my favorite inspirational quotes to help me focus my mind. Then, before I began studying, I would pray that God would help me to study and would help me to remember everything I studied.

To Join or Not to Join

As pledge day approached, I knew I was going to get a bid from one particular social fraternity. I wanted to join the fraternity and achieve the national status and presumed prestige that came along with being a part of that organization. However, I was worried because I had been to a couple of their rush parties. I knew that if I were to join that fraternity too many things would tempt me. Part of me thought that I could be a good witness to the other guys in the fraternity, but another part of me knew they might exert more of an influence on me than I would on them.

The night before bid day I couldn't sleep. I was up all night praying about my decision. The next day I attended the fraternity bid day ceremony and was given a bid, but I turned it down. It was a tough decision, but I didn't want to do anything that might cause me to slip up.

Psalms 119:9 says, "How can a young person stay on the path of purity? By living according to your word." I knew I couldn't put myself in any vulnerable situations and if I joined that fraternity I knew I would end up in circumstances I couldn't handle. Even King David, referred to in the Bible as "a man after [God's] own heart" (Acts 13:22), gave into temptation when he placed himself in vulnerable situations.

Later that year I did join a Christian fraternity, Beta Upsilon Chi (A.K.A. Brothers Under Christ). Joining that organization proved to be a great decision. My brothers encouraged me to do right and many of the friendships I made have lasted to this day. As a contrast, I witnessed two guys that where members of the other fraternity that I considered joining get kicked out of the university for behavioral issues.

Making the Grade

At the end of my second quarter at HBU I earned a 2.63 GPA (a "C+" average). I was excited that I passed all of my classes. I thought, "If I can just keep this up, I can graduate." I also discovered that when I started off the semester strong I wanted to finish strong. I didn't want to relax and throw away all the answered prayers and hard work that I had done at the beginning of the course. I wanted to keep going and make the best grades I could.

During the third and last quarter of my first year I made a 4.0—all "As." I couldn't wait to get home to tell my parents. I stopped at a pay phone somewhere between Houston and Dallas and called my dad. I don't think he believed me until he saw my grade report. I was so excited! I didn't think that I would ever be an "A" student.

One student at HBU that I looked up to was Justin Pankow. He took his academics seriously. As president of the fraternity I joined, Justin was the first student I spoke to at HBU. Disciplined, with integrity and humility, he earned the respect of every person that knew him. After I earned a 4.0 he told me it would become additive. He was right. It was the first of several 4.0 quarters. However, after my first one, I went back home for the summer and thought I was pretty smart. I got a little proud and thought I could knock out an anatomy and physiology course in a one-month term at a community college. I studied hard, but after failing the first test I had to drop the class. It was a reality check for me. I should not have enrolled in that class. I had not even taken introduction to biology yet. The experience reminded me of the importance of learning to take baby steps before running and to not think of myself more highly than I ought.

At the end of the summer, I received a call from the resident director of the men's dorm at HBU. He said that one of his resident assistants (R.A.) quit on him and asked if I would like to be a R.A. This opportunity was an answer to prayer. This position covered my room and board and allowed me to earn a little spending money. I accepted and before returning to school I chose a guy named Ross Shelton as my roommate because he was serious about being a good student. I wanted his study habits to rub off on me. Almost every time I entered the dorm room he was at his desk studying. He once told me that he worked to make his studying an act of worship to God. Watching him motivated me to study. Not only that, but he kept good habits and routines. He didn't stay up all night and he went to bed at a sensible hour. When his alarm went off in the morning he got up. I never saw him hit the snooze button. When he watched TV he preferred programs on current events, history, or world news. Every morning he went to the library to read the local daily paper and the Wall Street Journal.

Had I chosen a roommate that stayed up all night, slept in every morning, rarely studied, and played video games all day, I think that person would have influenced me differently than having a roommate like Ross. If I had picked a roommate with bad habits I'm sure it would have had a negative impact on the type of student I became. Fortunately, I didn't.

Another phenomenon occurred when I returned to school that fall. Some of my peers began asking to be in my group when we were assigned group work. Others asked to look at my class notes. I couldn't believe it. I used to be the one always asking to see other people's notes and now people were asking to see mine. The first time someone asked to see my notes I thought, "They must think I'm smart." It was an incredible feeling. Those remarks increased my confidence and made me want to work harder.

> **Work toward what you are asking God to help you with.**

I wasn't perfect, but God truly began to work in my life. I experienced His power when I trusted Him and worked toward what I was asking for (an effective combination). As I began to mature and seek God's will for my life, He began to open doors for me. God began to bless my life far beyond anything that I could have ever imagined. By the time I graduated from HBU, I earned a Bachelor of Arts with a double major in psychology and sociology, and received the President's Award, among many distinctions, along the way.

I want to share these awards with you, but not so you can say what a good man I am. I want you to know what God can do with the life of a boy who at one time didn't want to live, a boy who felt dumb and had been made fun of for not doing well in school. (See page 137 for the list.)

I never thought I would graduate from college. I never thought I was smart enough or had the discipline to earn a college degree. I thought that since I had ADHD I would never be able to overcome the challenges that come with that, but with God's grace and help I was able to earn a degree and more. Becoming a good student didn't happen overnight and there were many challenges along the way, but God saw me through it all.

At the end of the year, my roommate Ross Shelton also received the President's Award. Tiles with our names were placed side-by-side on the Walk of Honor at the University. Proverbs 27:17 says, "As iron sharpens iron, so one man sharpens another." The is a great example of the truth that you become like the people you hang around.

CHAPTER SEVEN

The Next Big Step

After graduating I moved back up to the Dallas area and a month later, in the summer of 2001, I married Gina, the girl that broke up with me before I went to HBU. My father performed the service. We began dating sometime after I moved to Houston and we kept up a long distance relationship for nearly three years while I was there.

Looking back, I know it was best that she wasn't able to relocate to Houston, even though she had tried. If she had moved to be near me, I would have spent more time with her and less time studying and being involved in leadership positions on campus. I believe I needed that separation and time alone to focus. God used that time to mature and develop me in a way that I would not have experienced otherwise.

Nonetheless, that first summer after graduating was a challenge. Married life took a little bit of an adjustment. Being married can be complicated, especially if you go into marriage with unrealistic expectations. Many times I wondered if I had married the right person. I'm sure she did, too. Before I got married I asked my dad how to know you're marrying the right person. The message he left me with was clear: While it's important to properly select your mate, it's also important to keep the commitment you make to the person you choose. Fortunately for me, my wife is very forgiving. Through her example, I learned a lot about grace. I do believe one of the reasons God created the institution of marriage was to show us how selfish we are and to use marriage to mold us to be more like His son Jesus. What I have learned is this: If you don't give up, if you submit to God and to each other, marriage can be a beautiful partnership and the love between the husband and wife will grow. I am fortunate and blessed to have a wife committed to marriage.

Follow the Right Path

I got the girl and lived happily ever after, right? Well, the ironic thing is that even after we got married there was a time that I again became depressed to the point of not wanting to get out of bed some mornings. The mind can be a battlefield, and I was letting my negative thoughts and regrets win and control me. I was at a point in my life where I wasn't sure what I was going to do with my life. I would let my mind wonder and think that because of some of my past mistakes, I had missed opportunities and I wouldn't be able to overcome the consequences of those mistakes. I wondered if I had missed my calling in life. After September 11, a million thoughts ran through my head. I had previously struggled with aspirations of going into the military, possibly the Air Force like my grandfather, and now I felt like I had made another wrong decision by not joining the Armed Forces.

> **Control your thoughts and emotions.**

Many days I was at the point where I didn't want to live, and I thought, "I'm not supposed to feel this way as a Christian; God has changed me." I let my unhappy thoughts become reality, and they were controlling me. My pessimism became a habitual cycle that took me in a downward spiral, creating a negative spirit. Thankfully, as sweet as she is, my wife is a tough woman, and she wouldn't let me feel sorry for myself.

Caught in a spiritual war, I wasn't in control of my thoughts as I should have been. I stopped doing the things that had helped me be successful. I was falling into old thinking habits, allowing my thoughts to control my feelings and emotions.

> **Keep doing the things that helped you achieve success in the first place.**

Once I achieved some level of success, I began to relax and back off the habits that brought me to a place of achievement. Change is a daily process and since we, as humans, are innately sinful, we must work each day at changing or we will revert back to our sinful nature. We have to continue to do the things daily that help us become successful in the first place. Thoughts lead to actions.

> **Think positive thoughts.**

As Paul encourages us to do in 2 Corinthians 10:5, I had to take charge of every thought to the obedience of Christ. Contrary to what some may say, positive thinking is Biblical. You might even say that God invented positive thinking.

Philippians 4:8-9 says, "Finally, brothers, whatever is true, whatever is noble, whatever is right, whatever is pure, whatever is lovely, whatever is admirable—if anything is excellent or praiseworthy—think about such things. Whatever you have learned or received or heard from me, or seen in me—put it into practice. And the God of peace will be with you." Also, Proverbs 23:7 says, "For as he thinks in his heart, so is he" (NKJV). Julian of Norwich, in her book Revelations of Divine Love wrote, "For of all the things our minds can think about God, it is thinking upon His goodness that pleases Him most and brings the most profit to our soul."

Time to Get a Job

While my wife had an excellent job when we got married, I wasn't able to land a full-time job for a while. That summer I mowed yards, trimmed bushes or did whatever work I could find. I wasn't lazy, but I wasn't exactly sure what I was supposed to do with my life. I wanted to earn a master's degree in counseling, but didn't put a lot of work into searching for a program. I visited a large public school in the Dallas/ Fort Worth area, but received little help on my visit and felt like they didn't really care about me or whether I attended their school or not.

Then I visited Dallas Baptist University (DBU). I had submitted an application the previous spring, but didn't complete any of the other paperwork. When I drove up onto the campus and parked I opened the car door and heard the bell tower chime playing Amazing Grace, my favorite song. That song has such special meaning to me. Not only can I identify with the words, but also with the author who experienced God's amazing grace on his life. John Newton wrote Amazing Grace. Before his conversion to Christ, he was an offensive, foul-mouthed sailor and slave trader. After his conversion, he experienced God's grace and left his old way of living to become a minister.

When I stepped out of the car onto University Hill I felt the presence of God on the campus. I didn't have to speak to anyone else. I knew that DBU was where God wanted me to be. The way I was treated by the staff only reinforced my decision. A staff member walking by noticed that I looked a little lost. He asked me if he could help and when I told him I was looking for the graduate office he stopped what he was doing and walked me there. My experience was so warm and inviting. The man I spoke with in the graduate office showed me all of the paperwork I would need to complete to be admitted. I felt the entire visit and experience was confirmation the LORD wanted me at DBU.

A few weeks later I found out I had been accepted to the university. I was ready and eager to start another phase of my life. While this was an exciting time, my wife was still wondering when I would get a job. One Friday morning she left for work and said, "You better have a job by Monday." I knew she meant it. By the end of the day I had a part-time job offer from DBU to work in the Office of Graduate Programs. I started a master's degree and my new job the same week.

Even though I never intended to stay in that position long, or to work in higher education, I felt I needed to work as hard as I could in that part-time position. I believe that when you work hard people will notice you and if they don't God does. I also believe that if you don't work hard people will also notice you, and you never know who might be watching.

I tried to pay attention to the little things like the way I dressed. I once heard that, when appropriate, you should dress for the position you want, not the one you have. While I was a student worker I wore a tie almost every day. Some people, including my immediate supervisor, asked me why I dressed up all the time. I wanted to appear as a professional and wearing a tie made me feel that way. On one occasion I happened to be in a meeting with the president of the university and he thanked me for always dressing as a professional at work. His comment confirmed two things for me: 1) you are being noticed even if you think you aren't, and 2) how you dress at work does make a difference. Even beyond that, dressing up has a psychological effect. Dressing up for work can make you feel more professional and, in return, perform more professionally.

When I started working at DBU I never really felt a "call" per say to Christian higher education. However, I do believe God led me to work on a degree at DBU, and He opened the door for employment there so I wanted to do the best job I could. I wanted to be known as a hard worker. That is something my father ingrained in me since I was a young child. I didn't want to let my family down, and I also knew that working hard was the right thing to do. I once heard my dad say in a sermon, "There is nothing unspiritual about hard work." I believe that.

Proverbs 10:4 says, "Lazy hands make a man poor, but diligent hands bring wealth." In 2 Thessalonians 3 Paul warns us about becoming idle and encourages us to work hard.

Strive to be the Best You Can Be

I learned to take control of the things I could, like dressing for the job, doing my best and giving over to God the things I couldn't. Chuck Swindoll once said, "How you perform at work will show people more about your relationship with God than how you worship on Sunday."

You can work in such a way to make your job performance an act of worship to God. Regardless of whether anyone else is watching or not, God is and how you work and what attitude you work with matters to Him. If you want to advance from point A to point B, you need to honor God with your work ethic. At the same time, ask God to prepare you for the next level, and pray that He will open the doors for you.

As a part-time employee I studied every brochure the university published so that I would be familiar with all the programs if asked about one by a prospective student. On more than one occasion this knowledge became useful.

> Make the commitment to do the best you can with what you have. Be the best you can be, striving to reach the full potential God has planted inside you.

Also it may be difficult to escape the politics people play, no matter where you work. People play politics in business, government, and unfortunately even in the ministry. I hate to say it, but throughout life you will find people who use religion to advance their own objectives and agenda. There will always be politics, but when you trust God you don't have to worry about playing the politics game. God is above politics. If you ever feel defeated by office politics just think of Psalms 46:1 which says, "God is our refuge and strength, and an ever-present help in trouble."

Wait on the LORD

Romans 8:25 says, "But if we hope for what we do not have, we wait for it patiently." When working and praying it's also important to remember that God's timing is not always your timing. Be patient in allowing God to not only prepare and develop you personally, but also to show the path ahead. When you take matters into your own hands and begin to manipulate situations, you run the risk of missing out on the best that God had planned. You may actually end up with less than God's best as a result of being impatient and not waiting on the LORD. There have been times in my life that I did not wait on God and tried to manipulate situations in my favor only to find out later that if I had waited God had something better in store for me. Right now it may be difficult for you to see a purpose and a plan for your life, given your current set of circumstances, but be patient. I promise you that if you walk before God with sincerity you will not be disappointed. But, if you jump ahead of what God is trying to do in your life, you could miss out on something incredible. Also, complaining about where you are in life does not honor God. Instead, work hard focusing on the things you need to do and allow God the time to make ready the path for you.

Once you receive a blessing from God it's also important to remember what is expected. Luke 12:48 says, "…For everyone to whom much is given; from him much shall be required…" (NKJV).

Work With a Sense of Purpose

I believed that I had been given much and much was expected of me. I knew that God had given me another chance at life and helped me complete a college degree, which at one time I thought was an impossible task. I couldn't sit back and rest on my accomplishments. I had a new sense of purpose and I knew much would be required of me.

I applied the principles I learned in Scripture to my work and after my first semester working part-time at DBU, I was offered a full-time recruiting position in another department at the university. I was grateful to have a full-time job with benefits, and my wife was happy as well. At first I didn't see my new job as a career. I viewed it as a means to help me complete an advanced degree and pay bills, but I worked as hard as I could anyway. 1 Corinthians 10:13 says, "So whether you eat or drink or whatever you do, do it all for the glory of God." I made it up in my mind that I would be the best recruiter that department ever employed, and maybe one day God would use it as a platform to give Him glory. It wasn't always easy. Recruiting can be tough work and many times I wanted to look for another job. I wasn't sure how recruiting students was helping to prepare me for my future career. Recruiting didn't have anything to do with my master's degree in counseling, which was the career I thought I would be pursuing.

Nevertheless, God continued to keep me at DBU so I did the best I could. I imagined my job as a recruiter as one of the most important, if not the most essential, position at the university. I would often tell myself that if I didn't do my job recruiting new students, there wouldn't be any other jobs at the university. If new students don't enroll, the university can't pay its staff, sustain programs, or continue. This way of thinking gave me purpose for each day at work. I believed my coworkers and colleagues at the university were depending on me. I wasn't sure how God would use this job in my life, but I wanted to work in such a way that I could use it as a platform to bring glory to

Him. Billy Sunday said, "More men fail through lack of purpose than lack of talent."

> **It's more important how you see yourself in your job than the job itself.**

Mark Sanborn, in his book The Fred Factor: How passion in your work and life can turn the ordinary into the extraordinary wrote, "The person doing the work determines the difference between the mundane and the magnificent." A.W. Tozer, in his book The Pursuit of God, said, "It is not what a man does that determines whether his work is sacred or secular, it is why he does it. The motive is everything."

After my first semester as a recruiter, I booked more recruiting events and received more prospect cards and applications for admission than any other recruiter in the recent history of the department. I worked with a greater sense of purpose than solely recruiting students. I strove to please God and to show him how grateful I was for the work He had given me.

Stay the Course

Halfway through my master's degree, I began to have doubts about a career as a licensed professional counselor. I wasn't sure counseling was what I wanted to do anymore. I still wanted to earn the degree, and I thought that maybe these were momentary feelings. I thought it could be possible that, by the time I completed my degree, I would want to be a counselor. I also knew that I couldn't always listen to my feelings because they could deceive, mislead, and betray. (If you don't master your feelings your feelings will master you.) I believed God had brought me to DBU to work on a counseling degree and that He had a plan for my life. If that was all the reason I had it was the right one and all I needed. I knew He would use the experience.

For the time being, I kept faithful with my education and my work, not knowing exactly how they would be used in the future. I believed God would work out the details, but in the meantime I believed He wanted me to remain where I was and do a good job. Even though I was getting a little antsy, I pressed on. My father's advice had always been to "stay the course." I believe that if you are sincerely and actively pursuing God's calling on your life then where you are is where you are supposed to be. In another one of Mark Sanborn's books, The Encore Effect: How to Achieve Remarkable Performances in Anything You Do, he says, "Until you find your purpose, continue to do things purposefully with energy and intention. When you do… sometimes the purpose will emerge."

Around this same time I read a book by my friend and DBU professor Dr. Dave Arnott titled Who MADE My Cheese? The book is a rebuttal to the best seller Who Moved My Cheese? In Dr. Arnott's book he encourages persistent production over looking for new "cheese." I resolved that continuing the course and working hard with what I had been given and entrusted was what I needed to do. Instead of looking for a new job, I needed to work hard at the one God already gave me and when He was ready, He would move me on.

Encouraging words can be found in Galatians 6:9, "Let us not become weary in doing good, for at the proper time we will reap a harvest if we do not give up."

CHAPTER EIGHT

Between the Big Moments

I was still working at DBU, but now two promotions later I was serving as director of student recruitment at DBU's northernmost regional academic center. When I had about a year left to complete my master's degree, my employer encouraged me to move to an area north of Dallas to be closer to the universities northern operations. My wife and I discussed the decision and prayed about it.

We decided to make the move and bought our first home in the summer of 2004. While we didn't know much about the area and would have to leave our church home to make the move, we wanted to be obedient and did so on faith to what we felt called to do. That decision turned out to be one of the best decisions we ever made. We live in a great community with so much opportunity.

About six months after we moved and right before the start of my last semester in my master's program, my wife and I had our first child, a daughter. It was a wonderful experience, and I felt so completely undeserving to be a parent. Scripture tells us, "God cast our sins as far as the east is from the west." Once God forgave me He no longer held my past against me. I was free to experience and enjoy an abundant life in Christ.

> ## Don't dwell on the past.

In our new community we now had the chance to attend Chuck Swindoll's church and did so for some time. The church's marketing department asked to photograph my family to use in promotional pieces for the church. The pictures were used for several years. Thinking back to those days I listened to Chuck's sermons on the radio for encouragement while driving to junior college, I never imagined that my future family would one day be used in his church's promotional pieces. It's amazing how God works. God truly redeems and restores.

In May, 2005, I completed a master's degree in counseling. It was an exciting time for my family because it seemed like such a huge accomplishment, considering the academic challenges I faced growing up. I was so grateful to God for having brought me through so much and for helping me to overcome those challenges. However, by this time I knew I did not want to be a professional counselor. Instead, I thought I should start looking for a sales position outside of DBU, and I began praying about my next move. There was a part of me that felt like I had missed the boat. It seemed like all my friends were way ahead of me in their careers. Most of them had finished college in four years—it took me six—and had landed terrific jobs right out of school. I was 28 years old, had worked for DBU recruiting in various capacities for four years, and still didn't know exactly what I was supposed to do in life.

Fortunately, I recalled that a couple of years prior to this point Dr. Arnott introduced me to the concept of FISO, an acronym that stands for "Fit In Stand Out." Basically this concept states that in order to be successful and find fulfillment in your work, you need to find an organization that you "fit in" and one in which you can also "stand out" in a good way. I felt like DBU was a great organization to work for and one that I felt like I "fit in." I had worked hard and hoped that I stood out. I wasn't sure if there would be a next step for me at the university, but I continued to work hard and pray for God to open doors for me, either at DBU or within another organization.

Three months after completing my master's degree, I was promoted to be the director of DBU's northern and largest regional academic center. In most cases, people that were older and had much more experience fill this position. At the same time, I began as a teaching adjunct through the College of Professional Studies at DBU. The learning curves at my new job and in teaching were tough, and I was thrown quite a few challenges along the way. Some days I wondered if I was in the right place, but I continued to work hard and trust Jesus to lead me. I kept in mind 1 Timothy 4:12 which says, "Don't let anyone look down on you because you are young, but set an example for the believers in speech, in life, in love, in faith, and in purity."

> We aren't promised work will be easy, but
> with the right attitude work can build
> character in your life.

Be Prepared

God planted in me a desire to pursue a doctorate degree and I searched for the best program. I finally found a program I felt was perfect. By the grace of God I was accepted into a doctorate program at the University of Alabama at Tuscaloosa. I was set to begin classes in the summer of 2007, just following the first birthday of our second daughter. I set a goal to finish the doctorate degree before my oldest child started school. (I didn't want to have to miss out on any of my children's school and extracurricular activities due to my studies.) The program set-up allowed for me to travel for a few days a month to attend class. This permitted me to continue working at DBU, and God provided for me to pay for my doctorate program. I've heard it said that "where God guides He provides." When God calls you He is always faithful to enable you to fulfill that calling.

I felt I was beginning to experience situations unfold that God had been developing when I wasn't sure how things would turn out. At the age of 30, I was named by Frisco Style Magazine to a short list of "People to Watch." (It was a nice feeling to receive this kind of recognition within the community.) That summer I was also promoted to the position of an assistant vice president at DBU while retaining my position as director of the regional academic center.

> Hard work pays off.

I continued to work hard and took a full course load each semester. I enrolled in 12 credit hours each fall and spring semester and nine credit hours in the summer terms. Many nights I went on four or less hours of sleep due to the amount of homework from my doctoral courses. Some nights I might not go to sleep until 3:00AM. Other mornings I would wake up at that time to study.

Trying to complete a doctorate degree with a full-time job, a wife, two kids and another one on the way was a completely different animal than when I was studying as a traditional-age student. Sometimes I was forced to break my own rules on studying, mainly getting plenty of sleep each night. I was trying to be responsible and faithful with all that had been entrusted to me, but there were times I felt like I might not be able to make it. I knew, however that I had been given a great opportunity and I might not get another like it so I would not let my mind cultivate any thoughts of quitting.

I would often think of my father and how hard he worked to earn a master's and a doctorate degree. Some nights he would be typing a paper when I went to bed and was still typing when I woke up. During the night he would put a typewriter and chair in a closet so that he wouldn't wake us up. I knew that if my father was able to sacrifice and work that hard, I could, too.

I believe God gave me supernatural strength to be able to go on such little sleep. Isaiah 40:29-31 says:

> He [the LORD] gives strength to the weary and increases the power of the weak. Even youths grow tired and weary, and young men stumble and fall; but those who hope in the LORD will renew their strength. They will soar on wings like eagles; they will run and not grow weary, they will walk and not be faint.

I made other commitments that I also wanted to keep. I remained active in my community, serving on various boards and participating in worthwhile community activities. Then, in the spring of 2008 the Collin County Business Press named me one of "21 Leaders for the 21st Century." (Collin County, noted as one of the wealthiest and fastest-growing counties in the United States, is home to corporate headquarters of JC Penney, Intuit, Dr. Pepper Snapple Group, Frito Lay, Rent-A-Center, Pizza Hut and many others.) This was truly a surprise and an unexpected honor.

The following spring at the age of 32, I was in my last semester at the University of Alabama, about to wrap up my 66-hour doctorate program and defend my dissertation. The semester was nearing an end when I found out the Dallas Business Journal had named me to their list of "40 Under Forty." This award recognizes forty successful people under the age of forty in the Dallas/Ft. Worth Metroplex (a combined population of nearly six and a half million people).

Faithful Parents

On May 9, 2009 I graduated from my doctorate program, and my parents were able to attend my graduation in Tuscaloosa. There were a lot of reasons why I couldn't and shouldn't have completed a doctorate degree, but there was one reason why I could and that was Jesus—the only reason that really mattered. That weekend, while attending the various graduation events and ceremonies, I reflected on how grateful I was to the LORD for giving me another chance and an opportunity to make my parents proud after I had caused them such grief. For years I had brought upon them such disappointment and shame. For years my parents had cried out to God on their knees, begging Him to work in my life. Their tears of frustration, sadness, and grief had now turned into tears of joy and happiness. I could see how pleased they were with me, and I was thankful God gave me an opportunity to make my parents proud. The work that God has done in my life is a testimony to the continued daily prayers of my faithful parents. My mom had spent so much time crying out on her knees before God for her son struggling in school, and now she and I both were reaping the fruit of her faithful prayers.

Not long after my graduation my mother sent me an email and in the message she told me about an experience she had in 1998 and said:

> I don't think I told you when you were in junior high after I would drop you off at school I would go home and lay across my bed with my Bible open and begin to pray for you. I did that several times a week. I don't know if you ever realized how painful it was for me as a parent to see you struggle academically. I know I was not the parent I needed to be to you at times and I am truly sorry, but you were always in my heart and I was constantly praying for you. I didn't know what else to

do at times but pray. I really loved you and felt very guilty for not being the mature mom you needed. I remember when we lived in Southlake as I continued to pray for you one day I sat on the floor at the foot of my bed and was praying for you. I sat there very frustrated with the Lord and just couldn't figure out why God was not answering my prayers. I felt God encouraging me to start praising him for what he was going to do in your life so I did at that point and that's when I really saw God start to move in your life.

1998 was the year I enrolled at Houston Baptist University and the same year God really began to take me through a dramatic transformation. God's goodness is humbling to experience and I'm reminded of the last half of Romans 2:4, that God's kindness can lead us to repentance.

I don't know where I would be today without my parents' prayers over my life. I know how fortunate I am to have such faithful parents and that not everyone may have praying parents. However, we do have a loving father in Jesus Christ who sits at the right hand of God and intercedes on our behalf (Romans 8:43). If your parents aren't the type that will pray for you, Jesus will when you call out to Him.

Above Self

After graduation I had about a month before I would take on the role of President of the 85-member Frisco Rotary Club, a secular organization with a motto of "Service Above Self." This was a volunteer position and something I was looking forward to doing. The role proved to be a lot of work, but it was very rewarding. At the end of 2009, I was also given additional responsibilities at the university. Then, in January of 2010 at the Frisco Chamber of Commerce's annual celebration, I was named Frisco's 2009 Citizen of the Year. Coincidently, According to the U.S. Census Bureau, Frisco was the fastest growing city in the U.S. in 2009 for cities with a population over 100,000 and the fastest growing city of the decade in the United States. In 2011, I became chairman of the Frisco Chamber of Commerce and we exceeded 1,000 member organizations that year.

I could never have imagined God would have blessed me like this. I'm sure those who nominated and voted for me on these awards never knew I had been asked to leave my high school. I shouldn't have received any of these awards. I've broken every one of the Ten Commandments, but God completely forgave me when I sincerely asked for His forgiveness and repented before Him.

I never thought I deserved a family. I thought I didn't deserve a child, but God has restored my life completely. I've been blessed with a wonderful wife, two beautiful daughters and a handsome son. Being a parent is one of the greatest privileges I've ever had. In my darkest days, I never dreamed that God could turn around my life like this. I got a late start living for Christ, but He made up for all the time I wasted, for all the time the devil tried to steal away.

I was so overwhelmed. I felt so undeserving. I'm nothing special. As a matter of fact, I deserve death. Life isn't always fair and praise God it's not, otherwise we would all have to hang on a cross. I've often wondered why God has shown me such favor. I may never find the answer. Being egocentric by human nature, I may be asking the wrong question. Perhaps it has more to do with the work God is doing and less about me. The work God has done, and is doing, in my life and in the lives of so many others is to bring Him glory. I once heard a speaker describe humility as not thinking less of yourself, but thinking of yourself less. As John the Baptist said, "He [Jesus] must become greater; I must become less" (John 3:30).

More of Him, Less of Me

After I received the citizen of the year award I started thinking to myself, "What do all these awards and accomplishments mean?" The more I thought about those questions, the more I continued to come back to the answer that it is all about God and bringing glory to Him. There is no other reason. Giving glory to God is our purpose on earth.

I don't believe God saved me from myself so that I could be happy. Happiness in and of itself is not the goal. We experience happiness and joy by doing the will of God and through a focused and committed relationship with Him. Dr. Henry Cloud, in his book The Law of Happiness, says, "Happiness is a by-product of living life as God designed it to be lived." Paul gave us an example of how our attitude should be when Christ saves us. We should be as bond servants to Christ. We should do our best for the purpose of glorifying God.

I've given invocations for business and political events involving presidents of major corporations, mayors, state representatives, senators, and congressmen. Each time I always pray in the name of Jesus. How could I not mention Jesus' name when I pray? He is on the only reason I'm alive and have the opportunity.

> **Keep in mind that your life is a testimony and that others are watching you. This will help hold you accountable and will motivate you to continue to work at changing and achieving great things.**

It doesn't matter if you're from the wrong or right side of the tracks, if your hands sweat, if your teeth aren't straight, if you're losing your hair, if you're handicapped, if you suffered through a terrible divorce, or whatever other excuse you can think of for not achieving the dream God has planted in your heart. It's not about what you can do, but what God can do through you. He doesn't ask you to do what you can't do; that's where He comes in. God just asks you to do what you can and He'll do what you can't.

Obstacles are nothing to God. He can enable you to overcome any barrier that you think might stand between you and achieving something great and reaching the full potential God has placed in you. You can become a champion for Christ and help others become champions for Christ as well.

Dead to Sin, Alive in Christ

When I made a decision to follow Christ, God never waved a magic wand to fix all my problems. I still had to work hard, but God did bless me and gave me favor that I otherwise would not have experienced apart from a relationship with Him. God gave me a fresh start. Then He removed all my guilt and shame, which were hindering me from moving forward in life, and gave me the confidence to move ahead and to pursue a full life. Through meditating on God's word, I was able to discover purpose. Even if I didn't know the exact plan, He gave me the drive to do my best in life for His glory.

God wants us to have a full life. In John 10:10 Jesus says, "The thief comes only to steal and kill and destroy; I have come that they may have life, and have it to the full."

Not surprisingly, the success I encountered increased my confidence, but not in the way that you might think. All the awards I received felt great when I received them, but the feeling wore off and left me wondering what it all meant. After reflecting on everything for some time, I realized that when I remain in Christ my confidence is not in myself, but in the LORD. I have little confidence in what I am personally capable of, but I know that through Christ all things are possible. Success has never fulfilled my life, but a relationship with Jesus Christ has. I realize now, more than ever, that my salvation and my strength are in Jesus Christ and through Him anything and everything can be accomplished. I can never earn enough awards, gather enough treasures, or attend enough parties to make my life feel complete otherwise. If you're searching for fulfillment you'll never find it in things on earth. You'll only find it through a relationship with Jesus Christ.

King Solomon had tried everything this world had to offer. He had wealth, real estate, servants, and over 700 wives. In Ecclesiastes 2:1-11 Solomon said:

> I said to myself, "Come now, I will test you with pleasure to find out what is good." But that also proved to be meaningless. "Laughter," I said, "is madness. And what does pleasure accomplish?" I tried cheering myself with wine, and embracing folly—my mind still guiding me with wisdom. I wanted to see what was good for people to do under the heavens during the few days of their lives. I undertook great projects: I built houses for myself and planted vineyards. I made gardens and parks and planted all kinds of fruit trees in them. I made reservoirs to water groves of flourishing trees. I bought male and female slaves and had other slaves who were born in my house. I also owned

more herds and flocks than anyone in Jerusalem before me. I amassed silver and gold for myself, and the treasure of kings and provinces. I acquired male and female singers, and a harem as well—the delights of a man's heart. I became greater by far than anyone in Jerusalem before me. In all this my wisdom stayed with me. I denied myself nothing my eyes desired; I refused my heart no pleasure. My heart took delight in all my labor, and this was the reward for all my toil. Yet when I surveyed all that my hands had done and what I had toiled to achieve, everything was meaningless, a chasing after the wind; nothing was gained under the sun.

At the end of Ecclesiastes Solomon sums up, "Now all has been heard; here is the conclusion of the matter: Fear God and keep his commandments, for this is the duty of all mankind. For God will bring every deed into judgment, including every hidden thing, whether it is good or evil."

Only by the grace of God can I do anything at all. Romans 12:3 says, "For by the grace given me I say to every one of you: Do not think of yourself more highly than you ought, but rather think of yourself with sober judgment, in accordance with the measure of faith God has given you." Ephesians 2:1-10 says:

As for you, you were dead in your transgressions and sins, in which you used to live when you followed the ways of this world and of the ruler of the kingdom of the air, the spirit who is now at work in those who are disobedient. All of us also lived among them at one time, gratifying the cravings of our sinful nature and following its desires and thoughts. Like the rest, we were by nature objects of wrath. But because of his great love for us, God, who is rich in mercy, made us alive with Christ even when we were dead in transgressions—it is by grace you have been saved. And God raised us up with Christ and seated us with him in the heavenly realms in Christ Jesus, in order that in the coming ages he might show the incomparable riches of his grace, expressed in his kindness to us in Christ Jesus. For it is by grace you have been saved, through faith—and this not from yourselves, it is the gift of God— not by works, so that no one can boast. For we are God's workmanship, created in Christ Jesus to do good works, which God prepared in advance for us to do.

Jesus has been my savior and redeemer. Metaphorically speaking, God has truly restored the years the locust have eaten (Joel 2:25). Matthew 6:33 says, "Seek first the Kingdom of God and his righteousness and all these things will be added unto you."

> **What you do in-between the big moments in life counts.**

I realize now that after I became a Christian I was still putting things before God. He wasn't trying to hurt me when He was working to take things out of my life that I put before Him. God had to remove those idols and break me down to a point that I would rely on Him for all my needs, including confidence, affirmation, and love. God was working to develop my character. Just like a vinedresser has to prune off branches, there were things in my life that God had to prune. While it can be a painful process, once pruned the plant will produce more fruit as a result. God has given me back many times more than I ever had to give up for him.

There have been times in my life I've had thoughts of quitting or giving up because the challenges were tough, but I didn't want to make a fool of God or let down all those that have prayed for me or that might be looking up to me. After my life turned around, I knew I had been given a chance to be a role model for others. I didn't want to throw away that opportunity or cause others to stumble. All of that held me accountable. When I thought about slacking off or doing something I shouldn't be doing I would think about how it would affect my testimony for Christ or my ability to minister to others. I wasn't always perfect, but that focus kept me out of a lot of trouble.

Staying focused, being consistent, working through adversity, and trying to do the things you need to be doing on a daily basis are keys to achieving successful outcomes. All of the awards and recognition I've received has been enjoyable, but it's what we do in between the big moments in our life, whether people are watching or not, that will ultimately define us.

PART THREE
A BETTER WAY TO THINK AND LIVE

CHAPTER NINE

A Different Path

> Read and meditate on Scripture and get
> to know the heart of God so that you can
> know His will.

I t is very easy for me to identify with the psalmist David because like Him I have committed some horrible sins, but when I humbly go before God, He is eagerly waiting to forgive me.

Psalms 103:1-13 reads:

> Praise the LORD, O my soul: All my inmost being, praise his holy name. Praise the LORD, O my soul, and forget not all his benefits - who forgives all your sins and heals your diseases, who redeems your life from the pit and crowns you with love and compassion, who satisfies your desires with good things so that your youth is renewed like the eagle's. The LORD works righteousness and justice for all the oppressed. He made known his ways to Moses, his deeds to the people of Israel: The LORD is compassionate and gracious, slow to anger, abounding in love. He will not always accuse, nor will he harbor his anger forever; he does not treat us as our sins deserve or repay us according to our iniquities. For as high as the heavens are above the earth, so great is his love for those who fear him; as far as the east is from the west, so far has he removed our transgressions from us. As a father has compassion on his children, so the LORD has compassion on those who fear him.

I also believe that when David mentions "diseases" in the passage above, it's not exclusive of depression, low-self esteem, drug addiction, or anything else you may be struggling with.

Listen very closely. I have experienced the hope and power of God in my life, and I want you to experience the same hope and power a relationship with Jesus Christ offers. Life does not have to be a dead-end road. Put your hope in God because He changes lives.

You may be going through a difficult situation right now, and it may be hard to see how any good could come out of it, but take heart. God can use any circumstance to accomplish His purpose. In Romans 8:28 Paul says, "And we know that in all things God works for the good of those who love Him, who have been called according to his purpose." Don't feel defeated, just keep moving forward. Love God and pursue His will and purpose. Don't let a negative situation be the end of your life story.

> **Keep moving forward.**

In the book of Job we see a man who lost everything, and he had a lot to lose. He lost his family, his livestock, and even his health, but through it all he continued to praise God. Job was even encouraged by his wife to curse God and die. That would have been a sad ending to his life, but that's not the ending Job wanted. Job feared God, and continued to worship Him in the midst of life shattering circumstances. In the last chapter of Job, we see that because of Job's faithfulness, God blessed him with twice as much as he had before (Job 42:10) and blessed the latter half of his life more than the first (Job 42:12).

Both King David and Job held a healthy reverent fear of the LORD. I learned to fear God, but not because I think He is out to get me and is always looking for the bad I do or that He wants to punish me. I fear the loss of His hand of protection and His favor on my life. I know what my existence was like before I trusted Him as my savior. I don't want to go back to that miserable lifestyle. A good healthy fear of God keeps believers in check. Not only that, but Scripture tells us that those who fear the LORD will be blessed.

Fear God.

Psalm 128:1 says, "Blessed are all who fear the LORD, who walk in his ways." There are many more verses in the Bible that talk about fearing the LORD. Psalm 121:1 says, "Praise the LORD. Blessed is the man who fears the LORD, who finds great delight in his commands." Psalm 25:12 says, "Who, then, is the man that fears the LORD? He will instruct him in the way chosen for him." Proverbs 31:20 says, "Charm is deceptive, and beauty is fleeting; but a woman who fears the LORD is to be praised."

I also know that since I am a child of God He loves me. I fear that if I become disobedient toward God that He will discipline me because of His love for me. I am grateful for His discipline, but if I can avoid it by being obedient to Him I will. That is a healthy fear of God. Proverbs 3:11-12 says, "My son, do not despise the LORD's discipline and do not resent his rebuke, because the LORD disciplines those he loves, as a father the son he delights in."

Choose to be Happy

God wants us to think optimistic and uplifting thoughts because He knows whatever we focus on we will become. Actions follow thoughts. As you think, so will you act. If you want to be positive and happy, you have to think positive and happy.

The difference between thinking positive thoughts as a Christian and in other worldviews is that in Christian positive thinking Christ is at the center. He is the reason why you choose to think positively, whereas the secular model is a "self-help" technique with the self at the center. Christ is the only reason anyone can have hope and the only reason we can be positive. Self-help methods are egocentric and the self cannot save. Instead of an egocentric mentality our attitudes should be God-centric with Christ being the reason for our positive thoughts. Charles Spurgeon, a Baptist preacher who lived in London in the 1800s, said, "The greatest enemy to human souls is the self-righteous spirit which makes men look to themselves for salvation."

Frank Minirith, M.D. and Paul Meier, M.D. wrote a book titled *Happiness Is a Choice*. The 200-plus-page book has a lot to say, but the premise is that you can be happy if you choose to be so. If you opt to be depressed or upset, you will be depressed and upset. If you decide to worry all the time you will only stress yourself out. Matthew 6:27 (NIV) says, "Who of you by worrying can add a single hour to his life?"

> **If you choose to focus on the good and to think and meditate on things that are positive, you will radiate a positive disposition, and people will want to be around you.**

You can choose to think about all the bad in life or you can decide to think about all the good in life. If you select to focus on all of your problems, people will most likely not want to hang around with you. After all, who wants to be friends with a grump?

You can focus on what you can't do or you can focus on can do. Either way your outlook, attitude, and overall demeanor will resemble your thoughts. How you think coincides with how you feel and vice versa; there is a direct correlation. If you want to feel better, think better. In essence, happiness is more a state of mind than a set of circumstances. I've heard it said that happy people don't have the best of everything; they make the best of everything.

Clinical psychologist and author Dr. Henry Cloud said, "Happy people set limits on what they will and will not allow in their lives." If you don't want to be negative, don't allow negative people or things in your life. Likewise, if you want to be positive, place positive people and things in your life. Put friends around you that will speak truth in your life. Don't waste your time hanging around people that are always putting you down. Negative people feed off of each other. Instead of hanging around people who tell you how dumb you are, put yourself around people who will encourage you and say positive things about you. Hang around people that will build you up. Most people will live up to or down to the expectations of others. If you want to be good put yourself around people who expect you to be good.

There are a lot of things in life you can't control. You have no control over who your parents are, what your age is, your skin color, whether you are born male or female, but you can control your attitude. You can choose to be a positive thinker. If you want to be a winner you've got to think like one. If you want to be successful you've got to see yourself as a winner and no longer a loser. 1 Corinthians 15:57 says, "But thanks be to God! He gives us the victory through our LORD Jesus Christ."

> **Don't focus on your failures, focus on what you want to achieve.**

Jesus has already paid the price for us as believers to be victorious over life. As I began to see myself the way God saw me, as a winner – and not as the person I use to be – my life began to pick up more momentum. Consider the message of the following poem:

Watch your thoughts; they become words.
Watch your words; they become actions.
Watch your actions; they become habits.
Watch your habits; they become character.
Watch your character; it becomes your destiny.

~Anonymous

In their book Telling Yourself the Truth, William Backus, Ph.D. and Marie Chapian, Ph.D. discuss what they have coined as Misbelief Therapy. This brand of therapy encourages clients to take on a new way of thinking. Some people get stuck in negative thoughts, which over time becomes a cycle in which the person is trapped and thinks pessimistic thoughts all the time. The authors suggest that clients break the habit of negative self-talk by speaking truth into their lives. Some examples of thought pattern changes listed by the authors include the following:

Instead of thinking "I am dumb" think "Thank you, LORD, for giving me intelligence."
Instead of thinking "I am unattractive" think "Thank you, LORD for making me attractive."

Instead of thinking "I have no talents" think "Thank you, LORD, for the talents you've given me."

Instead of thinking "I'm lonely" think "Thank you, LORD, for the friends I have."

Instead of thinking "I am miserable" think "I'm content."

Instead of thinking "I'm poor" think "Thank you, LORD, for making me prosper."

> **It's not always what happens to you; rather it's your perception of what happens to you that makes the difference.**

Proverbs 15:15 says, "All the days of the afflicted are evil. But he who is of a merry heart has a continual feast." Romans 12:2 says, "Do not conform any longer to the pattern of this world, but be transformed by the renewing of your mind. Then you will be able to test and approve what God's will is—His good, pleasing and perfect will."

Many times the situation you may think you are in is not reality, but your misbelief of the situation. Instead of allowing yourself to be afflicted by negative thoughts, be grateful for what you have. In other words, quit your "stink'in think'in" and choose to be positive.

Faith Can Move Mountains

Changing your thought patterns isn't easy and requires some work and a conscious effort on your part to think in more positive spiritual terms about life. Remember that God can and will work in and through you. Philippians 4:13 says, "I can do everything through Him who gives me strength."

If you want to increase your faith, you have to work at increasing your faith. You can exercise your faith, and thus increase it, through reading the Bible, spending time in prayer, tithing, serving others, witnessing and testifying to God's love, and trusting God in all situations.

God wants you to live a victorious and successful life. God isn't hoping that you will fail in life. He loves you and you are important to Him. He has conquered this world and life and wants you to be an heir in His kingdom.

> **Believe that God will work in you and do not doubt.**

James 1:5-8 says, "If anyone lacks wisdom, he should ask God, who gives generously to all without finding fault, and it will be given to him. But when he asks, he must believe and not doubt, because he who doubts is like a wave of the sea, blown and tossed by the wind. That man should not think he will receive anything from the LORD; he is a double-minded man, unstable in all he does."

Matthew 17:20 says, "I tell you the truth, if you have faith as small as a mustard seed, you can say to this mountain, 'Move from here to there' and it will move. Nothing will be impossible for you."

I've witnessed Jesus move some metaphorical mountains in my life. I experienced God give me the strength to fight off some lions and bears. Things have happened that seemed impossible, but through prayer and faith in God the impossible was performed.

What I believed about God and how He saw me was important in shaping my understanding of who I am in Christ. If I had believed that God was always looking for the bad in me, and waiting to catch me messing up, my life might have taken a different route. We can never do enough good to earn God's love. Likewise, we can never do enough wrong to lose His love. It's not something we earn, but rather a free gift we can either accept or reject. Thankfully, my parents helped develop in me a belief that Jesus loved me unconditionally, which was only strengthened by Scripture passages such as John 3:16-21:

> For God so loved the world that He gave His one and only Son, that whoever believes in Him shall not perish but have eternal life. For God did not send his Son into the world to condemn the world, but to save the world through Him. Whoever believes in Him is not condemned, but whoever does not believe stands condemned already because he has not believed in the name

of God's one and only Son. This is the verdict: Light has come into the world, but men loved darkness instead of light because their deeds were evil. Everyone who does evil hates the light, and will not come into the light for fear that his deeds will be exposed. But whoever lives by the truth comes into the light, so that it may be seen plainly that what he has done has been done through God.

Submit Your Life to God

Graduating from college can be mentally tough for students because they have been working toward an education for so long. Then, after it is over, they are supposed to become whomever they have been working toward becoming. Unless they have a job already lined up, they may feel as if they their identity is lost. For most of their lives, they were known as students. Now people are expecting them to be someone.

I struggled with who I was and what I was going to become. I had my doubts, and I think that played a major role in my depression. I began to realize that when I had those feelings of depression I had to hand it over to the LORD. If I didn't, I would have gone crazy. I couldn't have carried that burden by myself. But God can.

Philippians 4:6-7 says, "Do not be anxious about anything, but in everything, by prayer and petition, with thanksgiving, present your requests to God. And the peace of God, which transcends all understanding, will guard your hearts and your minds in Christ Jesus."

You don't have to try to live life solely through your own strength. You can trust in the power of the Holy Spirit to enable you to get through difficult times. Place your worries, fears, and anxieties in God's hands. As some have put it "let go and let God," but be sure you know how to let go and what that really means.

Graduating students aren't the only ones that struggle with this. I meet with people almost every day who are trying to figure out what they are supposed to do with their lives. I believe that, regardless of their age, most people struggle with discovering who it is they are supposed to be or what it is they are to be doing. Many people want to do significant things and others feel as though opportunity has passed them by.

> **Make an impact for Christ where you are today.**

One thing that helps me keep my focus is that if I am truly and sincerely seeking God, I believe wherever I am today is right where God wants me to be. God wants me to live out my Christian faith and to be a witness for Him today. You shouldn't worry about who you are to become and what you will do in the future more than who you are and what you are doing in the present. I'm not saying to not set future goals. Forming and working toward goals is good, as long as they are in line with God's will. I have set several goals for the future, and I practice writing them down. (I've found doing this to be an effective first step in achieving them.) However, tomorrow may never come or my goals may not be in God's will for my life.

So live in the moment for Christ because one thing is for sure: God can use you where you are today, no matter what circumstances you may find yourself in, as long as you are willing to submit your life to Him.

Working for Jesus

I believe that I am not working for my boss or for a company, but for Jesus Christ. If He has given me a job to do, I need to do it with all my might.

Colossians 3:23-24 says, "Whatever you do, work at it with all your heart, as working for the LORD, not for men, since you know that you will receive an inheritance from the LORD as a reward. It is the LORD Christ you are serving."

Always keep in mind that you are working for God and not for man. This will help you keep your attitude focused and it will make work more enjoyable when you experience difficulty. You won't get discouraged as easily when your boss doesn't recognize your hard work or when your boss or someone else takes credit for your work because you know that God is watching. God sees how hard you are, or are not, working. Remember, it's not man that can ultimately reward you, but it is God that will ultimately recognize and reward your attitude and work. If you work for your boss you will be disappointed when you don't get the promotion you wanted, but if you work for God you will earn a reward that will never be lost.

At the same time we are responsible for respecting the authority that God has placed over us. Romans 13:1-7 says:

> Everyone must submit himself to the governing authorities, for there is no authority except that which God has established. The authorities that exist have been established by God. Consequently, he who rebels against the authority is rebelling against what God has instituted, and those who do so will bring judgment on themselves. For rulers hold no terror for those who do right, but for those who do wrong. Do you want to be free from fear of the one in authority? Then do what is right and he will commend you. For he is God's servant to do you good. But if you do wrong, be afraid, for he does not bear the sword for nothing. He is God's servant, an agent of wrath to bring punishment on the wrongdoer. Therefore, it is necessary to submit to the authorities, not only because of possible punishment but also because of conscience. This is also why you pay taxes, for the authorities are God's servants, who give their full time to governing. Give everyone what you owe him: If you owe taxes, pay taxes; if revenue, then revenue; if respect, then respect; if honor, then honor.

We show honor and obedience to God by submitting to the authority over us. As hard as it may sometimes be to obey authority, remember obedience brings blessing. The alternative, disobedience, only brings burdens. In verse 13 of 2 Thessalonians 3, Paul tells us to "…never tire of doing what is right."

If you're ever struggling between doing what you know is right and doing what your flesh desires, keep in mind that being stuck between a "yes sir" and a "no sir" gives you an "ulcer." Indecisiveness will only increase your anxiety and stress. You can sure live with yourself better and sleep easier knowing that you've done the right thing.

Luke 16:10 says, "Whoever can be trusted with very little can also be trusted with much, and whoever is dishonest with very little will also be dishonest with much." My pastor once passed along some advice to me that was passed along to him, "If you're too big for the small things you're too small for the big things."

> **Be faithful in the little things.**

The Main Thing

Stay focused on the main thing. By purposing your life to live for Christ you can find meaning wherever you are and at any time. Each person you come in contact with may be a divine appointment from God; He may have placed that person(s) in your path for a very special and specific purpose that only you can accomplish. If you gear your thinking to treat each encounter you face as a divine appointment, you will begin to notice your perception and attitude for the things around you change. You may not be able to impact the entire world, but you can have an impact in your world. You can touch the life of each person you come in contact with for Christ.

Another phenomenon takes place when you stop focusing on yourself and begin focusing on others: You lose concern for your own problems or worries. You become concerned with meeting the needs of others instead of seeking out your own gratification. As a result, you will spend less time depressed over your own set of circumstances. You will feel grateful for your own situation when you realize what some other people live with.

Identity in Christ

Rather than placing identity in a job title or career, you should place your identity in Christ and who you are in Him. Jobs come and go, but if you remain in Christ what you do will last forever.

My significance does not come from what others think of me. I've had plenty of critics over my short lifespan and if I had continued to listen to them I don't know where I would be. What others do or don't say about me doesn't matter. My sense of worth and value doesn't come from praise or lack thereof. My value comes from Jesus Christ.

> **See yourself as God sees you,**
> **not as others see you.**

There have been times when I've been made to feel less than worthy by people. When I feel myself getting down because of comments made toward me, I pray to Jesus that I will only allow myself to get my feelings of worth from Him and not man. What God thinks of me is of much greater importance than what others think of me.

John 15:4 says, "Remain in me, and I will remain in you. No branch can bear fruit by itself; it must remain in the vine. Neither can you bear fruit unless you remain in me." If you want to live a fruitful life, you must place your hope and identity in Christ. If you do, nothing can take away what you gain.

CHAPTER TEN

Change is Possible

Yes, Jesus Christ provides a relationship that offers hope for change. 2 Corinthians 5:17 says, "Therefore, if anyone is in Christ, he is a new creation; the old has gone, the new has come!"

However, the redemptive hope Jesus offers is not just about us. Christ must be at the center of our motive. Robert McGee, in his book The Search for Significance says, "When self-improvement, rather than Christ, becomes the center of our focus, our focus is displaced." McGee also adds:

> The Christian life is not an easy one. It is not simply a self-improvement program. True, we may be able to make some changes in our habits through our own discipline and determination, but Christianity is not merely self-effort. The Christian life is a supernatural one in which we draw on Christ as our resource for direction, encouragement, and strength… The more we understand and apply the truths of justification, propitiation, reconciliation, and regeneration, the more our lives will reflect His character. Spiritual growth is not magic. It comes as we apply the love and forgiveness of Christ in our daily circumstances. It comes as we reflect on the unconditional acceptance of Christ and His awesome power and choose to respond to situations and people in light of His sovereign purpose and kindness toward us.

The Learning Curve

For years I thought that if I could just change the people around me, I would be happy. I tried to talk down to people and intimidate them. I talked down to my family, mostly my mom and sister. All that produced was resentment and bitterness. That will never work.

Instead, I must ask God to change me and be willing to change. Many people spend time trying to change their friends or family members when what they should be doing is asking and allowing God to change them. For years I mistreated my family thinking that I could change them, but that only created walls of separation.

Today, however, I can say that God has torn down those walls and relationships are being restored. I am closer to my family than I have ever been. Joel 2:25 says, "I will restore to you the years the swarming locust have eaten" (ESV). As the book of Joel tells us, if we sincerely turn from our sinful past and repent, God will transform and restore our lives because He is gracious and compassionate, "slow to anger and abounding in love" (Joel 2:13, ESV).

You can show your love for God by being obedient toward your parents. 1 Kings 3:3, "Solomon showed his love for the LORD by walking according to the instructions given him by his father David…" Also, God will bless you when you obey your parents. Ephesians 6:1-3 says, "Children, obey your parents in the Lord, for this is right. 'Honor your father and mother,' which is the first commandment [Exodus 20:12] with a promise, 'so that it may go well with you and that you may enjoy long life on the earth.'"

I cannot tell you how much trouble it would have saved me if I had listened to my parents while an adolescent, but I thought I knew what was best for my life and I wanted to have fun. The only problem was when it was time to pay the consequences for the bad choices I made the outcomes weren't very pleasant. For every action there are consequences and whether we like it or not we reap the consequence for our actions. Many times I had to find out for myself and learn the hard way. It took years for this law of actions and consequences to sink in for me. Many times I didn't fully think through the ramifications of my decisions before acting out. If something entered my mind, I acted upon it not giving thought to what might happen.

If you've had to suffer some severe consequences for poor decisions, know that God can restore what seems like the devil has taken away from you. He did so in my own life, but we must truly bow and repent of our sins before God. There were many days I spent with my face on the ground, repenting of my sin, asking God to forgive me and change me. God took all of my past failure and used it as motivation to help me be successful today. Because of my past failings I was motivated to prove to myself that, with God's help, I could be successful and prove to others that God changes lives. I did not want to let God or my family down when I knew I had been given a new chance on life.

As I began to witness the changes in my life that God was working on, I began to realize more His love for me. I started to understand that if God loves us He truly does want the very best for us. If this were true, then why would I want to do anything other than His will for my life? God's love for us doesn't mean His will for our lives will always be easy. But, it does mean that His will is best.

Fight Through Adversity

Many times the hard work, and adversity endured in difficult times, is the catalyst for a deeper and more mature faith in Jesus. Hardship may be the experience God needs us to go through to take us to another level with Him and to change us into the person Christ desires us to be. Throughout history there have been countless people that have had to endure and overcome enormous obstacles, but in the end they achieved great success.

One such example is Nick Vujicic. Born without any arms or legs, he wondered how a God who loved him could have created him that way. Nick was so depressed, lonely, and afraid of going through life he thought about committing suicide. He wondered what kind of purpose he could possibly serve.

But a renewed faith in God led Nick to realize that God did have a plan for his life. He wanted to use Nick to inspire others. With his new sense of purpose, he completed a bachelor's degree with a double major in accounting and finance. Today, Nick is the president of the international non-profit organization Life Without Limbs. He also founded his own motivational speaking company, Attitude is Altitude. Nick speaks all over the world and appears on televised programs sharing God's message of hope. Recently, he completed his first book. Nick's story is truly inspirational, but it didn't happen without faith in Christ and a lot of hard work.

To be a great athletic champion requires much effort. Only those athletes and teams that can overcome adversity will win the prize. In 1 Corinthians 9:24 Paul says, "Do you not know that in a race all the runners run, but only one gets the prize? Run in such a way as to get the prize." In 2 Timothy 4:7-8 Paul also says, "I have fought the good fight, I have finished the race, I have kept the faith. Now there is in store for me the crown of righteousness, which the LORD, the righteous Judge, will award to me on that day—and not only to me, but also to all who have longed for his appearing."

Run and don't stop. If you trip over a hurdle and fall, get back up and keep on running toward the prize.

A lot of people want to change but not everyone who wants to change is willing to put in the required work. You may need to separate yourself and move to a whole new environment. There may be some areas in your life that you don't want to give up, but you know you need to do so in order to live for Christ. There may be some friends you need to quit hanging out with or a relationship you need to leave, but you're scared, anxious, and unwilling to do so. You may think you won't find anyone else, but you could be missing out on God's best.

> ## Determine in your mind
> ## to change.

Fortunately, you don't have to make changes alone. God will help you and give you the strength to make the necessary changes.

It is all too easy to pray for God to bless us instead of praying for God to change us. However, in God changing us is the true blessing. As you begin to change your perceptions, ultimately situations also begin to change. Circumstances may seem hopeless, but there is hope in God. Obstacles may seem overwhelming but God can overcome them. You may be facing disappointment or disease and life may seem like a series of mountains, but God can help you climb them.

In John 16:33 Jesus promises us this world will be tough, but he also offers us comfort in knowing it will be all right; "I have told you these things, so that in me you may have peace. In this world you will have trouble. But take heart! I have overcome the world."

For God to begin a change in you all it takes is a sincere humble heart before Him. Matthew 23:12 says, "For whoever exalts himself will be humbled, and whoever humbles himself will be exalted."

Whatever it keeping you from a relationship with Jesus Christ, let it go. I tried a lot of what this world promised would bring me pleasure and even if it was fun for a while, it didn't last. The pleasure was temporary. My past choices caused me to miss some incredible opportunities because of the lingering consequences of those poor decisions. If only I had known then what I know now. An anonymous quote sums it up well: "Sin will take you farther than you want to go, keep you longer than you want to stay, and cost you more than you want to pay."

I learned to take responsibility for my actions because one day I will have to give an account for them. I once heard Dr. Jack Graham say in a sermon, "We are free to make our own choices, but we are not free to choose the consequences."

Nothing is worth missing out on what God has planned for you. Don't get discouraged, however, if you were like me and made some bad choices. God can redeem; I've experienced God's goodness. If I were to die today I would die a happy man. I have more than I ever dreamed possible and much more than I deserve.

Don't Miss Out

The time to begin living a fully committed life for Jesus is now. The time to do something is when you think of it.

Running from God and living outside of His will has its own set of consequences. Are you willing to accept those consequences? What is it you are holding onto that might be hindering God's blessing for your life? How much life, how many blessings have you already missed out on? Don't miss out on the abundant life God has to offer and live your life with more regret.

One of my favorite quotes is by an unknown author and it reads, "The Future is that time when you'll wish you had done what you aren't doing now." Five, ten, and twenty years from now you are most likely going to reflect back on your life. Are you doing what you need to be doing right now or will you look back with regret over the time you wasted? Are you willing to go through life not realizing the full potential God has placed in you? You may feel like you've made some wrong decisions that took you off course from God's will and calling for your life. Regardless of what you've done in the past, God can still do wonderful things with your life if you choose to live for Him now. When it comes time for the harvest, will you have planted any positive seeds that you will reap?

My friend and DBU professor Dr. Jim Underwood has written one of the best books on leadership I have ever read, More Than A Pink Cadillac: Mary Kay Inc.'s 9 Leadership Keys To Success. In the book, Dr. Underwood points out that Mary Kay believed: "It's not important where you start out, it's where you finish." Mary Kay had a rough start, but a fabulous finish. Her legacy continues today because her hope and self-worth was in God and not in what others may have thought or said about her. What kind of influence or message do you want to leave behind when you exit this life?

One of the things I regret the most is not living for the LORD when I was in high school. Among many other things I wish I would have been nicer to the "new guy" in school knowing personally what it felt like to be teased. I wonder what kind of affect I could have had on my peers had I been a positive influence instead of a negative one. While I can't go back in time I can make a difference now by influencing those I come in contact with each day. It would be awful to waste the opportunity to live for God now and the chance to positively influence those around me or do something great for God.

You may think you've messed your life up so bad that you couldn't ever correct it. You're right; you can't, but God can and He will restore you. Your sins don't have to define you. With God's help, you can reinvent your life. The greatest decision I've ever made was to live for Jesus. That decision changed the entire direction of my life. I need Him in my life and you do, too. We were made to live for Christ and glorify Him; in doing so you will find your true calling.

It's not too late to change. Don't think that you've missed your opportunity. You don't have to sit on the sideline of life thinking that you've done too much wrong or committed too many sins to ever be used by God. If you're alive God is not finished with you, and He can use you.

You can start right now. Your life can count. You can make a difference. You can do something meaningful with your life. Don't believe the lie or use the excuse that you're too old to change and make any real difference in the world or in the lives of those around you. There is no one else in the world like you, and there will never be another you. You were created with a special purpose and plan that only you can achieve. No one else was created to make the difference you were designed to make (Psalms 139:13-16).

In the book of Exodus, we read how Moses made some bad choices early on in his life, but God had a plan for him. It wasn't until Moses was more than 80 years old that God used him to lead the Israelites out of Egypt.

Don't think it's too late for your life. What you do in the second half of your life will tell more about who you are than what you did in the first half. You can begin living for Jesus now and make a difference. If God has planted a dream in your heart go after it with all you've got. God can use you no matter your age. He used a young boy named David to slay the armored Philistine giant Goliath with a slingshot. No matter how large the obstacle(s) you are facing may seem, remember that God is bigger. Life is not always about what you've achieved, but what you've had to overcome. 1 John 4:4 says, "You, dear children, are from God and have overcome them, because the one who is in you is greater than the one who is in the world." If you are in Christ, God can take back what the devil has stolen away from you.

> **Go after your dreams.**

Be a Doer

I know a lot of people who are very knowledgeable of Scripture. They quote verses all day long, go to church every time the doors are open, and always listen to Christian music in the car. But when it comes to actually applying Scripture in their life, they come up short.

James 1:22-25 says, "Do not merely listen to the word, and so deceive yourselves. Do what it says. Anyone who listens to the word but does not do what it says is like a man who looks at his face in a mirror and, after looking at himself, goes away and immediately forgets what he looks like. But the man who looks intently into the perfect law that gives freedom, and continues to do this, not forgetting what he has heard, but doing it—he will be blessed in what he does."

I realize that knowledge comes easier than application, but what good would it do an athlete to study good technique on film and then go into the sports arena and not put it into practice? In the same way, after studying God's word, we are to go onto the field of life and put His teachings into practice. Thomas á Kempis, author of Imitation of Christ, said, "At the Day of Judgment we shall not be asked what we have read, but what we have done."

Yes, being a doer will at times be difficult, but God's promises are real. Nothing is perfect, not marriages, families, jobs and certainly not the world we live in, but we have a perfect God who knows what is best for our lives. As much as I would like to be perfect, I am not and never will be while on earth. I make mistakes quite often. Many times I feel like Paul when he said in Romans 7, "I do the very things I do not want to do." Even now, years after having turned my life over to Jesus, I have made some dumb choices. I've done some things I should not have done and paid the consequences for my actions. It's easy for me to get frustrated with myself when I mess up, but I once heard a minister say that God has not called us to be perfect, just persistent.

The important thing is that when you fall down you don't stay down. Get up and move on. Ask God for forgiveness, turn from your sin, and don't allow Satan to hang feelings of false guilt over you. Praise God that He does not stop loving us or working in us just because we make mistakes. God loves us in spite of our mistakes.

Two wrongs don't make a right. When you mess up and ask God for His forgiveness, don't make the mistake of holding onto your failure. Doing so will only bring you down. Once you ask forgiveness, God remembers your sins no more. You've got to let go of your failure and move on. Don't spend time focusing on the wrong you've done, but rather focus on the good you want to be.

Time to Get Real

I am not naive enough to think that just because you may attend church or even because you may be a Christian you don't deal with some of the things I've mentioned. You may have a family member or friend that is struggling with similar issues. To those that are grappling with making a decision to give 100% of your life to Jesus: Don't let another day go by without saying "yes" to God. Nothing you desire could be greater than a relationship with Jesus Christ. If you need to make some changes in your life don't allow any more time to go by missing out on what God has for you. Let go of your pride and sincerely repent before God.

Fall Forward

If you're worried that you may look like a hypocrite if you decide to live for Christ and then mess up, it's too late. You already are a hypocrite; at one time or another everyone, Christian or not, is guilty of hypocrisy. We are all imperfect humans who are going to make mistakes, but remember you can recover from a fall.

The worst thing that can happen is not that you fail, but that you never try at all. You don't want to wake up one day and wish you had tried something you dreamed about doing. Mistakes are a part of life, but God's grace is sufficient to cover our sin and his love for us never decreases. However, God's grace is by no means an excuse to sin (see Romans 6), but His grace frees us so we do not have to live a defeated life. We can learn a lot from our mistakes, which can help us to live better lives and be all the more grateful for His amazing grace.

> **If you fall, fall forward.**

When you fall make sure you go forward and not backward. Falling forward means learning from failures and mistakes and growing into a better person because of those experiences. Falling backward means the opposite. When you don't learn from failures and mistakes you will most likely repeat them. When you fall backward you land on your backside. When you fall forward you land on your hands and knees. It's a lot easier to get up off your hands and knees than it is to get up off your rump.

Many people are so close to success when they give up. If only they could have seen around the corner. Perhaps if they knew success was almost within reach they might have had the strength to continue on. You may not know how close you are to succeeding. For you, success may be nearing. Persevere and continue forging ahead, doing what you believe God has called you to do. Remember Philippians 4:13: "I can do everything through him who gives me strength." When you're working hard, doing the things you need to be doing, extraordinary opportunities will come along, sometimes when you least expect them.

When Norman Vincent Peale completed his first book, numerous publishers turned him down. Thinking his work was a failure, he threw his manuscript in the trash and made his wife promise not to take it out. His wife did not listen and took the book to one more publisher. This time the publisher loved the book and renamed it The Power of Positive Thinking. To date the book has sold over 20 million copies and is printed in 46 different languages.

Don't Worry About What Others Say

Don't worry what friends will think or say about you. It doesn't matter. If Noah had taken the time to worry about what his friends thought of him building an ark out in the middle of the desert, he would have drowned along with them. You will always have critics. It's a fact of life. Not everyone is going to like you nor will everyone appreciate the work God does in your life.

In John 15:18 Jesus is recorded as saying, "If the world hates you, keep in mind that it hated me first." Jesus also tells us in Luke 6:22-23, "Blessed are you when men hate you, when they exclude you and insult you and reject your name as evil, because of the Son of Man. Rejoice in that day and leap for joy, because great is your reward in Heaven. For that is how their fathers treated the prophets." When people insult you or say bad things about you because of Christ just count it as stripes for Jesus.

There may even be some Christians who say the change isn't real. Don't worry about them. Just continue to do what you know is right.

There were some people in my church that made similar accusations about me after I decided to live for Christ. They said the change wasn't real. I don't necessarily blame them. I was a young Christian and still had a lot of maturing to do as a believer. However, I don't think they're talking now.

You can't control how other people will respond or what they say about you. People said all sorts of lies about Jesus when He walked on earth. He knows what it feels like to be falsely accused, but He didn't allow those lies to affect Him or deter Him from pursuing His purpose. I too have a responsibility to honor God and share with others the work He's done in my life. I can either answer that call or neglect it and miss out on fulfilling the mission of my life.

People who speak falsely about you, or do not believe God has changed you, need to check their own faith. They obviously do not believe in the full redemption God offers and are most likely missing out on grace and blessings from God. When people do say negative things about you don't sink to their level. In Luke 6:28 Jesus tells us to "bless those who curse you, pray for those who mistreat you."

Unfortunately, the truth is there will always be the doubters and people will say things behind your back or maybe even to your face. Let God handle those people. After the prodigal son came home and was shown love by his father, the prodigal son's brother became angry and spoke negatively about him (Luke 15:11-32).

Insults and gossip may begin with people you may least expect, like a close friend, a family member, or an employer. A minister may criticize you or talk falsely about the work God is doing in your life. You may not be able to do anything about others' attitudes, so don't allow them to bother you or get you down. Keep doing what you know is right. God's blessing on your life is not dependant on what your friends, your boss or others say or think about you. Focus on what it is that you need to do. Don't fall off course or allow others to discourage or distract you.

Keep On Keepin' On

Maybe you aren't like the prodigal son and you've lived your life for the LORD. You don't have to have a testimony of going off and doing your own thing and then coming back to God. If my friend, Aaron Crawford, had not been living his life for Jesus he would not have been there to pray with me. There's another story in this book besides the one about how God changed Jon Lineberger. There's a story about how Aaron Crawford was faithful to the LORD and how God used Aaron, a faithful servant, to help bring back a wayward sheep into the fold. Everyone should have a friend like Aaron. He wasn't embarrassed to call me his friend or hang out with me even though it could have damaged his reputation. He didn't agree with some of the things I was doing or participate in them, but when I was hurting he hurt with me. In my darkest time when I needed a true friend I turned to him.

No doubt Aaron had his own problems in life to deal with, but he took the time to care about me and be there for me. Aaron demonstrated God's love to me when I needed it most. You can be that faithful person who God uses to help someone turn his or her life around.

CHAPTER ELEVEN

Just as You Are

Don't listen to the lie that you must clean your life up before you come to Christ. If we all waited until our life was clean enough to come to God, we would never get there. God will accept you as you are and will help you mature as a Christian. You've got to start somewhere so start where you are. In Mark 2:17 Jesus said, "...It is not the healthy who need a doctor, but the sick. I have not come to call the righteous, but sinners."

The change in your life may not happen overnight and may take some time, but don't lose heart and keep your mind focused on the prize. Life is more a marathon than a sprint. In Philippians 3:12-14 Paul says, "Not that I have already obtained all this, or have already been made perfect, but I press on to take hold of that for which Christ Jesus took hold of me. Brothers, I do not consider myself yet to have taken hold of it. But this one thing I do: Forgetting what is behind and straining toward what is ahead, I press on toward the goal to win the prize for which God has called me heavenward in Christ Jesus."

God is not promising that life is going to be easy if you follow Him. On the contrary, in John 16:33 Jesus says, "In this world you will have trouble, but take heart! I have overcome the world." Life is still going to be challenging. I know. I've faced some tough situations as a Christian, but I can tell you that I am much happier living my life for God than I ever was living it for myself. There is nothing else in this world that I can put my trust in and find peace and contentment—not a job, money, possessions, not even a supportive network of people. Only Jesus can provide hope. When you're going through a difficult time as a Christian, God will not leave you.

Deuteronomy 31:8 says, "The LORD himself goes before you and will be with you; he will never leave you nor forsake you. Do not be afraid; do not be discouraged."

You still may have to walk through some difficult circumstances, but as a believer you no longer have to face life alone. In his book, *My Utmost for His Highest*, Oswald Chambers said, "God does not give us overcoming life: he gives us life as we overcome." In Luke 21:19, Jesus encourages us to remain strong when we face persecution; "Stand firm and you will gain life."

You are Here for a Reason

You are not reading this book by mistake. I believe that God wants to use you. The question is, "Are you willing to let Him use you?" Are you willing to ask and allow God to change your life? If you feel God is speaking to you, don't wait another moment to surrender your life completely to him. Don't miss out on the plans He has for you. God created you for a special purpose and plan. He made you with special gifts and abilities for a purpose that only you can fulfill.

Jeremiah 29:11 says, "For I know the plans I have for you," declares the LORD, "plans to prosper you and not to harm you, plans to give you a hope and a future." I like the way my childrens' New International Reader's Version Bible translates this verse, "I know the plans I have for you," announces the Lord. "I want you to enjoy success. I do not plan to harm you. I will give you hope for the years to come."

Commit all you do unto the LORD. Trust in Jesus Christ that He does have a better plan for your life than you do and fully surrender to His calling. Proverbs 20:24 says, "A man's steps are directed by the LORD. How then can anyone understand his own way?" As Proverbs 3:5-6 promises if we trust in God He will make our paths straight.

Unless you trust in God for guidance, you will never discover your purpose nor find your calling here on earth. If you want to be successful, submit to God and pursue His will for your life. Stop fighting it and be who God created you to be. There are a lot of things I would like to be, but they aren't me and they aren't who God made me to be. I will never be successful at them. Where I find peace, joy, and fulfillment is in surrendering to God and doing what I know He has called me to do. When you submit to be who God created you to be you can successfully carry out the purpose you were created for.

You may think that you are of no value to God, that God can't use you because you don't have all the right credentials. 1 Corinthians 1:26-31 says:

> Brothers, think of what you were when you were called. Not many of you were wise by human standards; not many were influential; not many were of noble birth. But God chose the foolish things of the world to shame the wise; God chose the weak things of the world to shame the strong. He chose the lowly things of this world and the despised things—and the things that are not—to nullify the things that are, so that no one may boast before Him. It is because of Him that you are in Christ Jesus, who has become for us wisdom from God—that is, our righteousness, holiness and redemption. Therefore, as it is written: "Let him who boasts boast in the LORD."

I know this is true because I experienced it. God doesn't need you to be well educated, come from a certain pedigree, or hold a fancy title. All He needs is for you to be willing to be used by Him and to obediently respond to His will and direction for your life. God will equip you along the way. He loves to use the ordinary to do the extraordinary; to turn tragedy into triumph. Don't use excuses like my hands sweat, I'm too young, I'm too old, my hair is falling out, my teeth are crooked, I face too much prejudice, I'm in a wheelchair, I don't have a degree, I've made too many mistakes, people don't respect me, or I have a horrible disease. Do those factors matter? Maybe they do to man, but at some point you have to say, "I'm not going to allow this set of circumstances to render me ineffective. I'm going to do the best I can with what I've got." You've got to take responsibility for what you do from here on out. God knows what is going on in your life. He can use it all for His glory and for the purpose in which you were created.

Life can be full of difficulties and disappointments and we all have our own set of problems to overcome. For instance, I shared an interest in a board position with an organization to one of the members on the nominating committee. He lightly patted me on the knee and said, "You're still young. You've got time." I could have let his reaction get me down. I could have said to myself, "No one takes me seriously. I look too young and no one will give me a chance. I'll need to wait until I'm older with more experience before I pursue higher positions." I could have taken on a bad attitude and been mad at the world for thinking too little of me or not giving me a chance. I could have been mad at God for making me look so young. Instead, I kept my focus doing the best I could and continued to work hard, believing that God has a plan for my life and how He made me look falls into that plan.

(Besides, it always helps to look on the bright side. There are many benefits to looking young. Recently, a door-to-door salesperson rang the doorbell of my house. When I answered she said, "Hi, are your parents home?" I responded, "No ma'am." She then asked, "Do you know when they will be back?" I answered her, "No, I don't." She responded back, "Okay then, I'll try back another time." I said, "Okay," and closed the door. It was the easiest out I've ever gotten—and I was honest.)

Maybe you have some serious challenges to overcome. Your challenges may seem insurmountable. You may wish you could start over because of the horrible mistakes you made in the past. For instance, I wish I had the testimony of the Heisman Trophy winner Tim Tebow, that of living a godly life throughout the teen and young adult years, being mature enough at an early age to make wise choices, and having the strong unfaltering determination to be a great football star, but unfortunately I didn't make the good decisions he did growing up.

There's nothing you can do about the past, but you can choose what you will do in the future. The most important thing is not how you start, but how you finish. You can choose now to finish strong. The theologian Carl Bard said, "Though no one can go back and make a brand new start, anyone can start from now and make a brand new ending."

Dr. Larry Crab, in his book, Inside Out, encourages his readers to focus on real authentic change from the inside by asking God to help change us. As authentic change begins to take place inside, it will be manifested on the outside. Change is a work in progress and doesn't happen overnight.

Yes, your past may not go away, but God is bigger than your past. The choices you have made have determined who you are today, but the choices you make today will determine who you become tomorrow. God can use your past, mistakes and all, for His glory. For me, my past and struggling with ADHD are what Paul might refer to as thorns in the flesh. In 2 Corinthians 12:7-10 Paul said:

> To keep me from becoming conceited because of these surpassingly great revelations, there was given me a thorn in my flesh, a messenger of Satan, to torment me. Three times I pleaded with the LORD to take it away from me. But he said to me, "My grace is sufficient for you, for my power is made perfect in weakness." Therefore I will boast all the more gladly about my weaknesses, so that Christ's power may rest on me. That is why, for Christ's sake, I delight in weaknesses, in insults, in hardships, in persecutions, in difficulties. For when I am weak, then I am strong.

My past and ADHD keeps me humble and grounded, knowing that my strength comes from God. I confess to pleading with God to take away the symptoms of ADHD, which have caused me so much frustration and anguish. I believe He could if He desired to do so, but for some reason God hasn't. Nevertheless, God's grace has been sufficient for me. The change in my life is not because of me, but Christ's work in my life. Only in Jesus can I boast.

God can give you success and He can take it away. With God it's not your success that is important, it's your obedience. Isaiah 55:7-9 says, "Let the wicked forsake his way and the evil man his thoughts. Let him turn to the LORD, and he will have mercy on him, and to our God, for He will freely pardon. 'For my thoughts are not your thoughts, neither are your ways my ways,' declares the LORD. 'As the heavens are higher than the earth, so are my ways higher than your ways and my thoughts than your thoughts.'"

God could have prevented me from experiencing a lot of the trouble and hurt I've gone through in life. While I was growing up my parents prayed that God would use me. Many times they didn't understand why I was experiencing some of the things I went through, but today I believe God allowed me to go through those distressing times so that I would be more empathetic to the lives of others and to be able to share a message of the hope and restoration God provides. There were times I wondered, and I'm sure my parents did too, where God was in the midst of such turmoil.

King David had the same question for God. In Psalm 139:7-8 David asks God, "Where can I go from your Spirit? Where can I flee from your presence? If I go up to the heavens, you are there; if I make my bed in the depths, you are there." I now realize that in my trouble God was there all along, allowing me to suffer through it all patiently knowing that one day He would use it and get the glory for bringing me out of it.

God's ways are not always our ways (Isaiah 55:8-9), and while you might not understand why you've experienced some bad things happen in your life, God can use brokenness to shape you and give you a different perspective on life. He may have allowed you to endure some trials so that you are better able to minister to others. Hang in there. While I wouldn't wish suffering on anyone, if it's handled in a godly manner, you will find that you can come out a much better person for enduring suffering in your life. Some of my most painful past experiences are the areas in which I am now able to minister to people the most. A.W. Tozer, in The Pursuit of God, said, "It is doubtful that God can use a man greatly until He hurts him deeply."

In Genesis 50:20 Joseph gives testimony to his own experience by saying, "You intended to harm me, but God intended it for good to accomplish what is now being done, the saving of many lives." Nineteenth century philosopher Henri-Frédéric Amiel was no stranger to suffering, having lost both of his parents when he was a very young age. While serving as a professor of moral philosophy at the Academy of Geneva, Amiel said, "You desire to know the art of living, my friend? It is contained in one phrase 'make use of suffering.'"

Strength in Weakness

While we may not understand it, God can take your weakness and past, and use it for His glory. Don't use your past as an excuse to think you can't become a new person in Christ today. You can start over with God's help. He can break the power sin may hold on your life. Don't let the world tell you who you are or who you will become. Don't let anyone crush your dreams or discourage you from pursuing your goals. Listen to Jesus and who He says you are and who He wants you to become. Don't live down to other people's expectations of you; instead, live up to God's expectations and desires for your life.

Too many Christians go through life and never fully experience God's grace and power. They may be too prideful to humble themselves before God, or too complacent with a casual Christian life. They settle for less than God's best. My friend Neal Jeffrey in his book, If I Can, Y-Y-You Can! said, "If you settle for a dream you can achieve in your own strength and intelligence, you will never experience what God can make of you and accomplish through you. If you allow your weaknesses and defeats to limit what you attempt in this life, you will miss the thrill of seeing God turn them into strengths and victories."

Don't feel like you can't come to Christ because He won't forgive you. You may be like I was, having made a lot of promises to God that you haven't been able to keep. You may feel that God doesn't trust you and won't listen to you or forgive you again. I once heard Dr. Charles Stanley say that God's willingness to forgive us is not motivated by our promises to Him. He forgives us because of His very nature and because of the sacrifice of Jesus Christ. He knows that we will never be perfect as long as we are on earth, but He still forgives us.

If you will sincerely confess your sins and repent before God, He will forgive you. No sin is so horrible that Christ cannot forgive it completely. 1 John 1:9 says, "If we confess our sins, he is faithful and just and will forgive us our sins and purify us from all unrighteousness."

Do you want your life to change? Do you want to set a new course? Are you willing to commit your life to Christ? It wasn't until I wanted to change and made a decision and commitment to live for Christ that my life began to transform. People could talk to me about living for God until they were blue in the face, but until I made a decision that I was no longer going to live for myself, but for Jesus and made the conscious effort to build a relationship with Him, did I begin to see my life change.

Are you the person you want and need to be? Are you just sleepwalking through life, complacent with the status quo? Have you been the witness you need to be to your family and friends? We are not promised tomorrow. Anything could happen to you, or a family member, or friend at anytime. You may think that one day you will do this or that, but frankly you may not make it to "one day." If you are thinking about living your life for Christ, make the decision to do it now.

You can't blame others for your decision not to follow Christ or pursue God's best. You may have been turned off or hurt by a family member, a close friend, a religious leader, or your church. This is between you and God. Regardless of what's happened in the past, this is a decision that you must make for yourself. Your life depends upon it. Blaming others for hurting you, or using the excuse that some Christians are hypocrites, is not going to work when you face Christ and give an account of your life. I could try to hold a lot of people or circumstances responsible for the things I did, but at the end of the day I am forced take responsibility for my actions.

Choose today to do what is right and live for Jesus. Don't throw yourself a pity party or begin to feel sorry for yourself or waste time getting depressed; these things can paralyze you and render you ineffective. Confess your sins and turn from your old way of life. Luke 16:13 tells us that you cannot serve two masters. You can't live for the LORD and live for yourself at the same time. Resolve today to live 100% for Christ and leave your old way of life. I can assure you that you will not regret it. I promise it will be the best decision you ever make.

Chapter Twelve

You Don't Have To Be Perfect

As long as you are still alive, it's not too late to start doing what is right and live for Christ. Here's what you need to do today: Begin to make good decisions and try to live a righteous life. While good works do not save you, your good works do prove your love for Christ and desire to live for Him. James said, "Thus also faith by itself, if it does not have works, is dead" (James 2:17, NKJV). He went on to say in verse 24, "You see then that a man is justified by works, and not by faith only" (NKJV). Also, in Titus 1:16 Paul says, "They profess to know God, but in their works they deny Him… (NKJV)."

Once you've made the decision to live for God, seek Him. Study His word and find out what He desires of His followers. On the inside of writer and preacher John Bunyon's Bible was written, "This book will keep you from sin, or sin will keep you from this book."

I believe if you stay in the Word and sincerely seek His will, God will direct, guide, and reveal Himself and His will to you. You may not know what God is doing in your life or what He is preparing you for, but continue seeking Him. Don't get discouraged if something doesn't work out the way you had hoped. Psalms 37:7-9 says:

Be still before the LORD and wait patiently for him;
fret not yourself over the one who prospers in his way,
over the man who carries out evil devices!
Refrain from anger, and forsake wrath!
Fret not yourself; it tends only to evil.
For the evildoers shall be cut off,
but those who wait for the LORD shall inherit the land.

We don't need to worry or try to manipulate situations in our favor. God takes care of the flowers of the field (Matthew 6:28). God has a plan for those that love Him and keep His commandments. Proverbs 16:9 says, "In his heart a man plans his course, but the LORD determines his steps." Believe and have faith that God has a plan for you and will reveal it to you in time. Hebrews 11:6 says, "Without faith it is impossible to please Him."

> ## You don't have to be perfect to change.

Being perfect isn't what the Christian life is all about here on earth. The disciples were less than perfect when God called them to follow Him. We can't hide anything from God because He knows us better than we know ourselves.

It was a year and a half after I decided to rededicate my life that I really began to get serious about school. Even then I still had many academic struggles. Becoming a good student didn't happen just because I wanted to be a good student. It took a lot of hard work and practice. While my heart had changed for the LORD I still had some bad habits I needed to work on. There were things I was learning and maturing in as a follower of Christ. I believe God allows us to endure the process of maturing because of the many lessons that are learned along the journey. These life experiences are one way we gain wisdom. God is still working on changing me every day.

Don't think you're too old or set in your ways to change. As long as you're alive you can begin to change. God will continually work to perfect you until the day you enter Heaven. Philippians 1:6 says, "Being confident of this, that He who began a good work in you will carry it on to completion until the day of Christ Jesus." We are all clay in God's hands. As followers of Christ we are continuously being shaped and molded. If you've ever worked with clay, you know that you want it to be soft and moldable. Hard clay is impossible to work with; it crumbles into pieces if you try to do anything with it.

Pray that you do not become hardened toward God or His voice in your life and that you will be moldable so that God can use you and work in you. Pray that your heart is soft to God's leading. Make an effort and a commitment to be teachable, coachable, and moldable.

> **Ask God to keep your heart from becoming hardened so that you can remain soft and moldable.**

Keep in mind that life can be difficult when trying to do the right thing and especially when others around you aren't. I'm not just talking about nonbelievers not doing what is right. I am also talking about those that claim to be Christians. Many times I have found that some Christians can influence you to do things that are not right. Some people I know who claim to be Christians act worse than people I know who are not believers. What they profess to believe isn't reflected in their actions. I've known some Christians with a horrible work ethic who steal from their employers. As believers we should be giving testimony to Christ through our work ethic.

Because we are human, we carry a sinful human nature. When Christians allow themselves to be led by their human nature or other worldly influences and not God they can commit some very wrong and sometimes painful acts.

The book of Psalms begins with this verse, "Blessed is the man who does not walk in the counsel of the wicked or stand in the way of sinners or sit in the seat of mockers." Keeping close company with nonbelievers or those that claim to believe yet live a very different life can influence you to take part in activities you should abstain from, especially when you are a new believer.

One Drink Too Many

Soon after giving my life to Christ I heard a quote that I wrote in the front of my Bible as a reminder. The quote reads, "The world says indulge thyself, the LORD says deny thyself." For me, alcohol is one of those indulgences I cannot handle and need to deny. After deciding to live for the LORD I gave up alcohol, but after being sober for some time I thought I was mature and strong enough to handle a glass of wine or a beer with dinner. Besides, according to some research, a glass of red wine is healthy. Scientists report that beer contains antioxidants. My one glass eventually ended up being two and two ended up being a bottle and before you know it, I was drinking way more than I should have. I liked the taste and feeling too much to enjoy just one glass of wine or just one beer.

While in John Chapter 2 Jesus turned the water into wine, it's hard to argue with verses in the Bible that teach us "not to get drunk on wine" (Ephesians 5:18). Proverbs 20:1 says, "Wine is a mocker and beer a brawler; whoever gets drunk on them is not wise."

I want to be wise and I've made a fool of myself one too many times because I drank too much. Due to my history with alcohol, I've decided it is best if I not indulge myself even in one drink; regardless of what zip code I'm in. Besides, you don't have to be a social drinker to be successful in business.

On one particular occasion I was at a reception where real estate legend Ebby Halliday was one of the speakers. At the time she was 99 years old and was asked the secret of her longevity. Ebby replied, "I don't drink, I don't smoke, and I don't retire." Later that evening I had the opportunity to escort Ebby out to her car and found myself impressed with her sharp mind. She had sung a little ditty during her speech at the reception, and on her way out she grabbed my arm and told me that she had written the words while she waited on her turn to speak during the program. There must be some truth to her secret of longevity. This reminds me of the oracle King Lemuel's mother taught him recorded in Proverbs 31, specifically verse 4, "It is not for kings, O Lemuel--not for kings to drink wine, not for rulers to crave beer."

I do not want to fall back into the same lifestyle I once had, and I feel that alcohol could lead me there. I don't want to start making bad choices, and I don't want to influence my children in a negative way. It would be a terrible tragedy and sin if my drinking influenced my children to become alcoholics or worse. Proverbs 23:29-33 says:

Who has woe? Who has sorrow? Who has strife? Who has complaints? Who has needless bruises? Who has bloodshot eyes? Those who linger over wine, who go to sample bowls of mixed wine. Do not gaze at wine when it is red, when it sparkles in the cup, when it goes down smoothly! In the end it bites like a snake and poisons like a viper. Your eyes will see strange sites and your mind will imagine confusing things.

I've also thought, "I have a family now; what if there were an emergency and I wasn't sober minded enough to make the right decision(s) or drive to the hospital if needed?" If I am to be the leader of my family, I need to always be prepared to take care of them in any situation. I am a complete nincompoop when I drink and usually end up embarrassing myself or doing something that I regret. When I tried to quit drinking before it was because I felt I had to, but I still wanted to drink. I now no longer drink because I do not want to drink. For the first time, I no longer crave alcohol or desire it, probably because my last experience was so embarrassing and I now recognize the important responsibility I have to represent Christ.

Besides, alcohol is a depressant and I don't need anything pulling me down. I am happier living for God than I ever was living for myself. My life doesn't need alcohol and there are other ways to maintain a healthy diet. I do think it is important to maintain good health and be a good steward of the body God has given us. We should take care of our bodies as they are the temple of Christ (1 Corinthians 6:19). However, we cannot put our hope in our life while on earth. 1 Timothy 4:8 says, "For bodily exercise profits a little, but godliness is profitable for all things, having promise of the life that now is and of that which is to come" (NKJV).

Our time is coming, and one day we will all die and give an account of our life. Are you ready for that day? Having to give an account for my life is one of the things that motivates me. I don't want to waste what time I have left on foolishness. It is worth repeating what Paul said in Philippians 1:21, "For to me to live is Christ, and to die is gain."

There may be some things you give up, but they might try to creep back into your life. Be on guard and don't be deceived. Stay the course and do the things you know you need to do to reach your full potential as a Christian and in life. Nothing is worth missing out on God's best plan for your life. Choose the best. God has shown us how to be successful. All we have to do to be successful is follow Him.

F.B. Meyer said, "We never test the resources of God until we test the impossible." Matthew 19:26 says, "Jesus looked at them and said, 'With man this is impossible, but with God all things are possible.'"

If you knew that you couldn't fail what is it that you would do? Because of all the tough times and good times I have been through, my faith in God and what He can do through me has strengthened. When there is something that I want to accomplish and believe God is leading me to do, I don't doubt. I just move in the direction I feel led in and keep moving until the door is closed. Sometimes the door closes and sometimes it doesn't. Regardless of whatever happens, I know that with God there are no accidents.

Perfect? Not a Chance

Avoid the temptation of perfectionism, which can lead to sin and unhappiness. After becoming a Christian I thought I had to follow a lot of rules. I fell for the trap of thinking I had to be perfect and that other Christians should be the same way. I looked down on other Christians when they made mistakes.

I set standards for others that I myself wasn't able to keep. Instead of focusing on the good, I started looking for all the bad in myself and in others. I seemed to always be disappointed. As a result, I spent a lot of time being unhappy. That kind of thinking is legalistic and can ultimately paralyze you from receiving and experiencing God's supernatural power and blessing. While there are set rules to follow, no one can perfectly follow them all. However, because of Christ's death and sacrifice on the cross we are free, through grace, from the bondage religious rules can have over us. Nevertheless, this freedom, because of grace, as Paul put it in Romans 6:1, does not give us license to go on sinning so that grace may increase all the more. As Christians we should strive for excellence, but if we stumble along the way we don't have to mentally or verbally come down hard on ourselves or others. We should confess our sins and then move beyond them.

Additionally, you can damage a lot of people and make them feel like they cannot be used by God because of some negative comment you might state. In the process, you will hurt your own witness. Paul also tells us in 1 Corinthians 13 that the greatest thing we can do is to show love to others. At times, this may require us to speak truth to someone, but we can do so in love and restore believers gently (Galatians 6).

The fact is that no one can ever be perfect while on earth. Because I am a perfectionist I was quick to beat up on myself and was crtical of others. I expected a lot from people and when they did not meet my expectations I was very judgmental.

A few years ago, however, I realized what I was doing and began working through it. It is so much better to appreciate, accept and love people for who they are. I once heard Dr. Charles Stanley say, "You can destroy a person's future with words." Everyone—myself included—will make mistakes. Now I know that things don't have to be perfect, and I don't want to be held responsible for shattering someone's future or dreams.

In If I Can, Y-Y-You Can!, Neal Jeffrey says, "Nowhere in the Bible does it say you have to do everything perfectly in order to experience God's power and miracles in and through your life." The Bible is full of stories about imperfect people that God used in spite of their imperfection. Paul wasn't perfect. Before his conversion, he went around persecuting and killing Christians. Yet we see how Paul, after a supernatural encounter with Jesus, began proclaiming the Gospel. God inspired Paul to write most of the books in the New Testament. Peter had no formal education and he is infamous for three times denying he knew Jesus. Still, knowing all this, Jesus called him the "rock." After Christ's resurrection, we never hear of Peter denying Christ again.

Dr. Jack Graham, in his book Powering Up says, "On more than a few occasions I've asked God the question, 'Is it really possible that I can achieve your mission when I'm this far from being perfect?'" Dr. Graham continues by saying, "The fullness of God's presence and power does not come through good deeds. It does not come through church membership. It does not come through growing up in a godly family. It comes my friend, only through salvation in Christ."

Here again, it's not about pedigree, social status, or title. It's about God. We are not perfect and we are going to make mistakes. Dr. Graham goes on to say:

So many believers stay planted on the spiritual bench because they have failed God in some way and wonder if the infraction will leave them permanently sidelined...They're living in defeat and at great distance from the God who created them and loves them, constantly teetering on the brink of spiritual despondency because they don't realize that with God's presence comes His promise to renew us day by day, to fire us up moment by moment. Regardless of our past. Regardless of our sin...when God uses people like you and me who are utterly undeserving and unworthy of being used, and he accomplished magnificent things through us, who do you suppose gets the glory? God does!

Forgive

Praise God that He can and will use us in spite of our imperfections, in spite of our past mistakes, and in spite of us being human. Our performance has nothing to do with God's grace. When you let go of the idea that people, especially Christians, have to be perfect you will enjoy yourself more for who you are, faults and all, and you will appreciate others for who they are. You will be much more accepting and forgiving of people when they make mistakes. Dr. Henry Cloud says, "When you forgive others, you are the biggest beneficiary." As Christians we have been forgiven much and we should be forgiving and show grace toward others, realizing that every Christian is a work in progress.

> **Forgive and ask for forgiveness.**

Avoid Jealousy

Resist the urge to compare yourself and your situation with that of others. What God may be doing in you and in someone else are two different things. Just because God worked one way in someone else's life, or because God blessed someone else in a certain way, doesn't mean you should expect God to work or bless you in the same way.

He may want to do something different in your life. If you allow your attitude to sour because you feel you've been cheated, or that God hasn't blessed you the way you think He should, you may end up missing out on the blessing of your life. While works do not get you into Heaven, your attitude and actions will set the stage for blessing in this life and/or when we, as believers, enter Heaven. Keep your focus on Christ and not your circumstances.

When I began changing my attitude about having to be perfect I became much happier and much more relaxed. Waiting for the perfect moment or conditions can paralyze you. Besides that, the perfect conditions may not exist, or at least not in the way you had imagined. When you keep in mind that most of life happens under less than favorable circumstances, it's much easier to accept your situation and do the best you can with what you've been given. On the flip side, if you wait around for the perfect opportunity you may wait all of your life and never do anything.

Go the Distance, Finish Strong

One day we will all give an account to God for how we spent the time, gifts, and talents that He blessed us with. In Acts 20:24 Paul says, "However, I consider my life worth nothing to me, if only I may finish the race and complete the task the LORD Jesus has given me - the task of testifying to the gospel of God's grace."

When our time on earth is nearing an end, some of us may have an opportunity to contemplate about what contribution(s) we might have made during our life. One day we will all leave behind a life message, a legacy. What will yours be? Don't die with your message untold, your song unsung, your gifts that God gave you unused. Your challenge is set. Will you rise to meet it?

If God has worked in your life, share what He has done with others. When you begin to share with others what God has done in your life you will begin to experience spiritual growth as a believer and hopefully encourage others by your story to live their life for Christ. While you will never be able to fully repay Christ, sharing with others how God has worked in your life is a way to give back out of love and gratefulness for what God has done in you. Psalms 107:2 says, "Let the redeemed of the LORD say so…"

There are a lot of people that have helped me along the way. I may never be able to repay them, but I can show my gratitude by helping others. After I became a Christian there were a few people I felt I needed to go to and ask for forgiveness. It was awkward and difficult, but afterward I felt much better and my conscience was clear.

To those who've been reconciled to God through Jesus Christ, He has given them the ministry of reconciliation (2 Corinthians 5:12-21). If God has worked in you it's now your responsibility and ministry to be Christ's ambassador and share with others the reconciling power of Jesus Christ.

If you haven't already, I hope that you will also make a decision to live your life for Christ and not look back, except only to be thankful for what God has done in your life and to appreciate how far He has brought you. Each day when I arrive at work, I can see from my office window both the rehab faciltiy I checked into when I was 18 and the church I am a member of today. It is a reminder to me not only of God's amazing grace and love, but also His supernatural power to change a life.

> **Make a commitment to live your life for Jesus Christ and make Him the Lord of your life.**

Consider each day of your life to be a brick. Just as a home is built one brick at a time, so your life is built one day at a time. Make each day count. If you do, years from now you will look back and be amazed at what God has accomplished through you and the beautiful life He has built one brick at a time. Don't allow the revival God is doing in your life to end. Stay committed to finishing strong and may you experience much success as you seek to follow Jesus Christ.

17 Truths to a Changed Life

Living life the same old way will not get you different results. If you want to change you've got to take responsibility for yourself and make some changes. To make changes you've got to start by making choices. The choices you make today will determine who you will be tomorrow. Life is about choices and if you want good results you've got to make good decisions.

The following 17 truths are meant to help guide you through the process of experiencing change in your own life. While I was not understanding of these truths when I first sought change, God revealed them to me along the way and gave me insight into each one. By no means are these steps a complete, exhaustive or comprehensive list, nor are they the only way by which God will work in your life. God works in us through both similar and different ways as evidenced by the examples, recorded in the Bible, of those God changed. The apostle Paul wasn't even considering a change in his life when he met Jesus on the road to Damascus.

However, if you know that you want and need to change, but do not know where to begin, these 17 truths offer some guidance. What is most important is that you give your life 100% to Christ and sincerely work hard to live for Him. If you get this right, God will guide you along the way and work to bring about change in your life.

The Truths

1. **You must want to change and be willing to do so.** Wanting to change is the first step and may be a sign that God is working in your life, but it's not enough to just want to change. Lots of people say they want to change, but few are willing to go the distance and even fewer are willing to take the necessary steps or make the needed adjustments. Go beyond the want to willing.

2. **Make a commitment to live your life for Jesus Christ and humbly make Him the Lord of your life.** Take the necessary steps to end your old way of existing and start a new way of living in Christ.

This may mean that you stop hanging out with your current group of friends or ending that relationship you know is neither healthy nor leading you closer to Christ. To be fully committed to Christ may also mean that you need to stop watching certain shows, listening to certain music, or participating in certain activities. Proverbs 16:17 says, "The highway of the upright avoids evil; those who guard their ways preserve their lives." Make the commitment to live for Christ; it's a decision only you can make.

3. **Pray and ask God to change your life.** We are sinful by nature so changing to be more like Christ is going to require help from God and is something you will need to work at daily. Ask God to keep your heart from becoming hardened so that you can remain soft and moldable. Asking God to change you can be difficult because there may be some areas that you know you need to change, but are afraid, for whatever reasons, to give up. Ask God to help you develop discipline in your life to do the right things. 2 Chronicles 7:14 is a promise and says, "if my people, who are called by my name, will humble themselves and pray and seek my face and turn from their wicked ways, then I will hear from heaven, and I will forgive their sin and will heal their land."

4. **Work hard toward what you are asking God to help you with.** You can't expect God to work in you or in a situation, if you are not willing to work toward what you are praying for. It's easy to say you believe, but your actions will tell the truth and prove either your faith or lack thereof. In James 2:14-26, James tells us that faith without works is dead. In other words, faith, if not backed up with action, is worthless. Work to develop self-discipline and good habits in your life. Working toward what you are asking God to do is a step of faith by which God can perform a miracle in your life. If you really want God to change you, do something about it! Back it up with action and work at changing.

As believers in Christ we live under God's grace, but there is nothing unspiritual about hard work. You cannot expect God to bless you if you're going to be lazy. Whatever you have to do today, do the best job you can. Blessings will sometimes come when you least expect them because you are working hard at the things you should be doing.

Colossians 3:23-24 says, "Whatever you do, work at it with all your heart, as working for the Lord, not for men, since you know that you will receive an inheritance from the Lord as a reward. It is the Lord Christ you are serving."

5. **Read and meditate on Scripture and get to know the heart of God so that you can know His will.** The Bible is one way that God speaks to us. Scripture is full of wisdom and when you read the Bible God will reveal Himself and His will for your life. Psalm 119:98-100 says, "Your commands make me wiser than my enemies, for they are ever with me. I have more insight than all my teachers, for I meditate on your statutes. I have more understanding than the elders, for I obey your precepts." As you meditate on God and His Word, just be still and listen for His voice.

6. **Put yourself around the right type of people.** It's not enough to simply stop hanging out with the wrong people. Place yourself around positive and encouraging people that want to live for Christ. Their good habits, values, and focus will be a positive influence on you. You will become like the company you keep.

7. **See yourself as God sees you, not how others see you.** People may think you are too young, not educated enough, and lack experience, or offer some other excuse why you cannot accomplish something. Most likely they are projecting onto you how they feel about themselves. Motivational speaker Zig Ziglar said, "You cannot perform in a manner inconsistent with the way you see yourself. If you don't see yourself as a winner, then you cannot perform as a winner." The shepherd boy David didn't listen to those who laughed at him or gave him reasons why he shouldn't fight or couldn't defeat the Philistine giant Goliath. He believed in God and trusted in what he felt the Lord was calling and preparing him to do. He saw himself capable of defeating the armored giant with only a slingshot because the Lord was with him. Don't let anyone else tell you who you should or shouldn't be. Listen to God and trust in Him to guide you as you faithfully act according to His prompting.

8. **Realize you don't have to be perfect.** It is not necessary to have a particular pedigree, attend the right schools, keep a spotless reputation, or know the right people. You just need to be willing to live

your life completely for God. All throughout the Bible you can read stories of imperfect people that God used to accomplish extraordinary things because they were willing to be used by Him.

9. **Keep in mind that your life is a testimony and that others are watching you.** This will help hold you accountable and will motivate you to continue to work at changing and achieving great things so that you can set a good example for others as a Christian. You don't want to be a stumbling block to others or have your actions give non-believers a reason to call Christians hypocrites. 2 Corinthians 6:3 says, "We put no stumbling block in anyone's path, so that our ministry will not be discredited."

10. **Don't dwell on the past.** There is nothing wrong with looking back and being thankful to God for redeeming you from your old life, but don't allow your past mistakes to bring you down. Also, dwelling too much on past successes and becoming complacent can also hold you back. I've known some very successful people that got comfortable with what they had already achieved and quit striving for more. Look to the future. Just like the Apostle Paul said, forget what is behind and press ahead toward the goal (Philippians 3:13).

11. **If you fall, fall forward.** Everyone makes mistakes. It is a part of life. Basketball coaching legend John Wooden said, "If you're not making mistakes then you're not doing anything. I'm positive a doer makes mistakes." When you do fall the key is to get back up, dust yourself off, ask for forgiveness if you need to, and continue moving forward. Don't allow guilt to render you ineffective. There's no time to sit around feeling depressed about your mistakes. Take care of them and move on, continuing to do God's work.

12. **Forgive and ask for forgiveness.** Why? Because God forgave us and most likely we will need forgiveness in the future. Forgiving is not only Biblical, it will also release you from a lot of psychological, emotional, and physical stress and free your mind up to allow you to be more productive for Christ. Not forgiving others can cause you to become bitter and you might speak without thinking. Holding in bitterness gives those persons you are bitter against control over your life because you are allowing them to still upset you and make you mad. If you don't want them to have control over you let it go. Forgiving

people will also win you respect. Proverbs 19:11 says, "Sensible people control their temper; they earn respect by overlooking wrongs" (NLT). Forgiveness is not a feeling. Forgiveness is a choice.

13. **Think and speak positively.** Change your thoughts, words, and attitude, and you will change your actions and ultimately your life. There are a lot of things in life that you do not have control over, but you can choose your attitude. The founder of the Ford Motor Company, Henry Ford, said, "Whether you think you can or can't, you're right." Believe that through Christ He can enable you to do anything. Pastor and author Robert Morris in his book The Power of Your Words says, "You can determine your future quality of life by the words you speak." You will hear a lot of talk, but the most important words you listen to are the words you tell yourself so practice positive self-talk.

14. **Set goals (write them down) and go after your dreams.** Setting a goal will help give you direction and writing it down can be an effective first step in achieving that goal. If there is something you feel God is leading you to accomplish, write it down and then go after it with all you've got. Until you write down your goal it's just a dream. I firmly believe, and have personally experienced, that writing down a goal is the first step to achieving it. Also, when setting a goal don't sell God short or underestimate what He can do in your life. Pray about what goals God is leading you to pursue and then go after the huge goals that seem impossible. That is when you will really see God work in your life.

15. **Believe and have faith.** Hebrews chapter 11 is a great passage on faith. The author of Hebrews defines faith in chapter 11 vs. 1 this way: "Now faith is being sure of what we hope for and certain of what we do not see." Later in vs. 6 the author says, "And without faith it is impossible to please God, because anyone who comes to him must believe that he exists and that he rewards those who earnestly seek him." In Matthew 17:20, Jesus said, "...I tell you the truth, if you have faith as small as a mustard seed, you can say to this mountain, 'Move from here to there' and it will move. Nothing will be impossible for you." In the story of Jesus healing the blind begging man Bartimaeus, as recorded in Mark 10:46-52, Jesus says to Bartimaeus, "What do you

want me to do for you?" Bartimaeus then tells Jesus that he wants to have sight. Jesus responds by saying, "Go, your faith has healed you" and immediately Bartimaeus was well. Jesus still performs miracles today just as He did while walking on the earth. You can be sure of that. Believe in God and trust that He can and will redeem, restore, and renew your life.

16. **Remain humble.** Scripture warns us about the harm associated with pride. Proverbs 16:18 says, "Pride goes before destruction, a haughty spirit before a fall." The Bible also tells us that God honors humility. James 4:10 says, "Humble yourselves before the Lord, and he will exalt you" (ESV). God may or may not take away your unhealthy or sinful desires and pride can often lead us to believe that we are deserving of the pleasure to indulge in such desires. However, humility practices the discipline of denying self. If you want to see God work in your life don't let your pride get in the way. Humble yourself before Him and He will indeed lift you up.

17. **Don't give up!** Keep on keepin' on and stay focused on the prize. Luke 21:19 says, "By standing firm you will gain life." Success is just around the corner. Some corners are longer than others, but if you continue to do the right things and stay on the right path God will bless you. No doubt you will face challenges along the way, but just like an athlete in preparation for a race visualize yourself crossing the finish line and accomplishing the goals God has for you. Keeping the end in focus will help you endure through the difficult times knowing that victory awaits you.

Awards and Recognition from College
(Mentioned from page 63)

Who's Who Among American Universities and Colleges
The National Dean's List
National Collegiate Social Sciences Awards Winner
National Collegiate Education Awards Winner
Inducted into the Psychology National Honor Society
An officer in the Sociology International Honor Society
Treasurer of Beta Upsilon Chi (Brothers Under Christ)
Served on the Student Judiciary Board
Served on the Ministry Leadership Council
Student Senate Chaplain and Chairman of Husky Leadership
    Conference
Voted 2001 Homecoming King
Voted 2001 Mr. HBU
Voted Senior Class Favorite
Received Presidents Award and had my name placed on a tile in
the Walk of Honor

The academic techniques God helped me develop are in my booklet, Tips for Academic Success in College: Habits that will make you a better student, available as a free PDF on my website www.jonlineberger.com.

Bibliography

Arnott, D. (2002). Who MADE my cheese?: A parable about persistent production (Writers Club Press: Lincoln, NE)

Backus, D. W. & Chapian, M. (2000). Telling yourself the truth (Bethany House Publishers: Minneapolis, MN)

Chambers, O. (1927). My Utmost for His Highest (England)

Cloud, H. (2011). The Law of Happiness: How spiritual wisdom and modern science can change your life (Howard Books: New York, NY)

Crabb, L. J. (1988). Inside out. (Navpress: Colorado Springs, CO)

Graham, J. (2009). Powering up: The fulfillment and fruit of a God-fueled life (Crossway Books: Wheaton, IL)

Jeffrey, N. (2009). If I can, y-y-you can! (Sampson Publishing: Dallas, TX)

Maxwell, J. (1998). The 21 Irrefutable Laws of Leadership: Follow them and people will follow you (Thomas Nelson: Nashville, TN)

McGee, R. S. (2003). The search for significance: Seeing your true worth through God's eyes. (W Publishing Group: Nashville, TN)

Meier, P. B. & Minrith, F. D. (1994). Happiness is a choice (Baker Books: Grand Rapids, MI)

Morris, R. (2006). The Power of Your Words: How God can bless your life through the words you speak (Regal Books: Ventura, CA)

Sanborn, M. (2008). The Encore Effect: How to achieve remarkable performance in anything you do (The Doubleday Publishing Group: New York)

Sanborn, M. (2004). The Fred Factor: How passion in your work and life can turn the ordinary into the extraordinary (WaterBrook Press: Colorado Spring, CO)

Tozer, A. W. (1982). The Pursuit of God (Christian Publication: Camp Hill, PA)

Wooden, J. & Jamison, S. (2005). Wooden on leadership (McGraw-Hill: New York, NY)